Maritime KENSINGTON

SHIPWRIGHT DYNASTIES OF PHILADELPHIA

GRETCHEN M. BELL

THE
History
PRESS

Published by The History Press
Charleston, SC
www.historypress.com

First published 2024

Manufactured in the United States

ISBN 9781467157292

Library of Congress Control Number: 2024941835

Notice: The information in this book is true and complete to the best of our knowledge. It is offered without guarantee on the part of the author or The History Press. The author and The History Press disclaim all liability in connection with the use of this book.

Dedicated to Rich Remer, who imbued me with his passion for the stories of the nineteenth-century shipwrights of Kensington, the family connections between them and the intriguing history they left behind.

CONTENTS

Preface   7
Acknowledgements   9
Introduction   11

1. The Lenapes, Swedes and English   15

2. Shipbuilding Begins   23

3. Anthony Palmer and His First Purchasers   26

4. The Norris, Lynn and Eyre Families   32

5. Shipwrights Bower, Brusstar and Grice:
    Steam Technology Comes to America   37

6. End of the Century: Early Shipbuilding Partnerships   42

7. Fitch and Evans   47

8. The Nineteenth Century: Kensington Shipyard Expansion   50

9. The War of 1812 and a Change of Focus for Philadelphia   55

10. The Beginnings of Cramp and the Rise of the Railroad   59

11. Transition Years at Kensington Shipyards   66

12. The Surviving Shipwrights Recover   71

13. The Zenith of Wooden Shipbuilding and
     Immigration Pressures   78

14. The Economic Panic of 1857 and Civil War   87

15. Neafie & Levy; Birely, Hillman & Streaker; and Cramp:
    The Last of the Kensington Shipwrights   97

16. The New Navy and the End of Cramp Family Ownership   107

Epilogue   119
Notes on Sources   123
Notes   125
Bibliography   133
Index   139
About the Author   143

PREFACE

My education on this subject began at Laurel Hill Cemetery. I had signed up for one of Dan Dailey's tours, "From Sails to Steel: Shipbuilders of Philadelphia," led by local historian Ken Milano. As he warned us to watch for the groundhog holes, Ken walked the group around to view the headstones of William Cramp, John K. Hammitt, Samuel Merrick, John Birely, John Vaughan and William Sutton, all while outlining their stories.

I was interested to learn more. I asked Ken if there were any books about the Kensington shipbuilding industry. He told me that a friend named Rich Remer was working on one and that he might need some help. Ken put us in touch with each other.

Rich had been researching the genealogy of Kensington ship tradesmen since the 1990s, beginning with his ancestor, caulker and shipwright Matthew Remer. He had also combed through city directories from 1785 to the Civil War and found the rise and fall of major shipwright clans evidenced there. Rich had the idea to extract shipwright family names and build a database to document these family fortunes. This we did.

I was working in the Penn Treaty Park building at the time, and I was completely unaware of the heritage of the land right outside the door. On visits to work with Rich, he took me back through time as he described the importance of the Delaware River shad to the Lenape tribe, Anthony Palmer's founding of Kensington, the Eyre brothers' involvement with the Revolutionary War and so much more. We were constantly exasperated at discovering wonderful details about people from Kensington who achieved incredible success but were not documented in histories of the region. Rich allowed me to borrow his files and lent many books that he thought I should read. As I learned about these shipwrights, and the forces that affected their craft, I knew that Rich Remer's project must be published.

The Kensington and Fishtown communities ought to know the history behind the names on their street signs, Philadelphians should appreciate their impressive industrial past and the East Coast must acknowledge the innovations that came out of the once world-renowned shipyards of Kensington.

ACKNOWLEDGEMENTS

Thanks to Mike Persa at the National Museum of Industrial History in Bethlehem, Pennsylvania, and Dr. Jay Moore and Gerry Hanley at Mariner's Museum, Newport News, Virginia, for proofreading my draft on early steamboat technology.

Through e-mail communication and an in-person visit, the staff at the G.W. Blunt White Library at Mystic Seaport Museum, Connecticut—Maribeth Quinlan, Patricia M. Schaefer and Paul O'Pecko—kindly searched their collection and found the Philadelphia Customs District shipwright certificates that were rescued, and then donated, by Marion V. Brewington.

I appreciate the assistance of Rich Remer's friends Dan Dailey and Ken Milano—Dan, a proud descendant of John Birely, gave me permission to include images from his incredible Kensington shipbuilding collection, and Ken initially introduced me to Rich Remer, shared Rich's files and answered my questions.

I made good use of the website philageohistory.org, created and maintained by Bruce Laverty and Adam Levine. Their Greater Philadelphia Geohistory Network is a wonderful resource.

A thousand thanks to Bob Bell for IT support, manuscript formatting, assisting with images and a partnership of forty years.

INTRODUCTION

The story of the Kensington shipwrights in the eighteenth and nineteenth centuries is a chronicle of the core group of families who settled there, occasionally intermarried, forged business partnerships and passed on property to heirs.

Surprisingly, there is an almost complete lack of literature regarding the early history of Philadelphia shipbuilding. As the maritime historian Marion V. Brewington said in an address to the Historical Society of Pennsylvania in 1939:

> *New York, Boston, or Baltimore, or even Nantucket, Salem, or New Bedford. All of them have publicized their maritime history to the utmost, while we here in Philadelphia for some unknown reason have entirely neglected it. Ours is equally as interesting, almost as ancient, and in some ways of even greater importance in national history.*

He also spoke of the difficulties of writing such a history: "To tell the whole story of maritime Philadelphia would be impossible. Much of its past has been irretrievably lost."[1]

Mr. Brewington could have been referring to customs vessel documentation or the physical remnants of the city's shipbuilding legacy. Both were lost. As Kensington ship construction declined terminally after World War II, the shipyards, wharves and associated structures were neglected. The decision to locate the I-95 interstate along the river was the final moment of disregard for the once-great Kensington shipwright community.

The city has a local organization known as Hidden City Philadelphia. I have admired its goal of drawing attention to places hidden in plain sight. I attended the Hidden City Festival in 2009 and 2013 and became aware of sites such as the John Grass Wood Turning Shop off Second Street and the Royal Theatre on South Street. "Hidden" connotes existing but hard to find. Demolished sites are, of course, nonexistent. With the tearing down of the Cramp Machine & Turret Shop on Richmond Street in 2011 to build an I-95 interchange, the last piece of Philadelphia's great nineteenth-century shipbuilding industry was gone. Just as I was learning about maritime Kensington, it disappeared completely. Elliott and Popkin, authors of *Philadelphia: Finding the Hidden City*, describe looking for markers to know what had been present. Street names were all the markers I had. Documents, deeds and genealogies had to re-create the story.

My trips to the National Archives led to a palpable sense of sorrow about how much is missing. I was interested in shipwright certificates, which were required on every ship launch. I discovered the NARA Bureau of Marine Inspection and Navigation on my first visit to Washington. I thought that I should go back to search the Mid-Atlantic Region of NARA, as the Philadelphia District Custom House had held this paperwork at one point. The archivist at the Mid-Atlantic Region offices and I discussed what I was looking for, and after a few hours in the Record Group 41 Section, she reported that the oldest vessel documents they held were from 1900. She contacted the D.C. NARA to ask its staff to go more specifically to RG 41, Custom House Records, 1789–1955, and an archivist responded that he did find one box of master carpenter and shipwright certificates.

When a researcher is informed that there is one box of material, sometimes one doesn't know what the dimensions of the container will be. When I received the "box," it was the size of a thin accordion file. When I pulled the top back, it appeared empty. Then I noticed two folders in the front. There were indeed master carpenter and shipwright certificates for the Philadelphia district—for ships built in Camden, Paulsboro, Trenton—as well as *one* certificate scribbled on blank parchment for the steamboat *Delaware* built by Joseph and Francis Grice in 1813. Sadly, I have to assume that Rich Remer's description of Custom House workers disposing of thousands of documents is true.

Why was this industry so ignored by historians? The lack of interest in retaining pieces of heritage relates to the politics of remembering the past and to Philadelphia's self-image. East Coast shipbuilding reputations were claimed through art and literature by New York's clipper ships and

New England whalers. Even though the nineteenth-century world moved everywhere via the water and merchants made their fortunes from the cargo traded by vessels, the shipwrights of Kensington were just a part of the developing industry north of the city. To be fair, Philadelphians didn't have a sense of their own history until events around the time of the founding of the Historical Society of Pennsylvania in 1826 focused the attention of citizens on preserving the past. And perhaps retaining ship documents was not considered important after the industry shifted to the Navy Yard in South Philadelphia.

I determined to restore the memory of these laboring clans who lived and worked along the Delaware River. I consider *Maritime Kensington* to be a general survey; it is the beginning of what I hope will be ongoing research on the subject. For this study, shipwright family histories were sought at the Historical Society of Pennsylvania, shipbuilding company archives at Independence Seaport Museum were searched and many books were perused at the Free Library. To write the "impossible" history, I have pulled together thousands of such threads and relied on our city directory database to give a skeleton outline of some of the shipwrights' lives.

Family networks were the basis of shipwright businesses in the early years of the industry in Philadelphia. Sociologist Daniel Bell described capitalism as not only an economic system but also a social system in which power is transmitted through family. He wrote that the social organization of the family rested on two institutions: property and the "dynastic" marriage.

Research revealed how often intermarriage resulted in a landless carpenter or shipwright acquiring Kensington waterfront property or a wharf—or both. A small business was built. Young sons and nephews were apprenticed in the business, and partnerships with similarly successful shipwrights were created. Early partnerships were very informal, temporary mergers.

This book will provide an account of how this industry evolved in Kensington, who the key shipwrights were and how their families came to build the wooden sailing ships and iron steamships that commanded worldwide respect for Philadelphia.

Chapter 1

THE LENAPES, SWEDES AND ENGLISH

Kensington is older than the city of Philadelphia itself. The name was given by Anthony Palmer to his estate. Palmer's property was in the old Native American settlement of Kackamensi, later anglicized as Shackamaxon, which had existed along the western shore of the Delaware River opposite Petty's Island.

The Delaware River, which the Natives called the Lenapewihittuck ("the rapid stream of the Lenape"), had many tributaries as great rivers do. The Tumanaramingo Creek was a navigable stream, the dry creek bed of which is buried under today's Aramingo Avenue in Port Richmond. The Cohocksink Creek had a serpentine path under the current-day Northern Liberty streets of Canal, Allen, Hancock and Laurel. The Cohoquinoque Creek ran from west to east. It remains as a sewer under Willow Street, which winds through the Callowhill neighborhood.[2]

The land on both sides of the Cohoquinoque Creek was low and swampy. South of this stream, the west banks of the Delaware rise abruptly to a height of about thirty feet above the river.[3] Between the Cohocksink and Tumanaramingo Creeks, there was a wide, sandy beach gently sloping up to rich meadow lands.

The Delaware Valley in the early seventeenth century was the ancestral home of the Lenni-Lenape Native Americans. These people lived on both sides of the Delaware River; along the east bank, they inhabited the land south of the Raritan River, and on the west bank they occupied the area as far north as Easton and south to the Delaware Bay.

The Lenapes migrated inland during the winter months to hunt, and when spring approached, they occupied settlements located near the mouths of creeks.[4] The Delaware tributaries likely provided the turbulent water that shad required to breed. Shad was one of the most important foods of the Lenape summer diet.

American shad are anadromous, meaning they are born in fresh water but live most of their lives in salt water. They are known to migrate long distances through the Atlantic and up rivers, staying in the mainstream and larger waterways to reach spawning grounds. Adult shad look for proper water flow, depth, temperature and bottom structure to lay eggs.

The shad lifecycle begins in fresh water when eggs hatch. The fingerlings spend several months in fresh water, reaching salt water by fall. As small fish, they spend four to five years feeding in the ocean and grow to about eighteen inches. At that point, they become sexually mature and make their spawning runs, returning as adults to flowing fresh water to reproduce. Shad eat little on their upstream run; they postpone eating for the downriver trip back to the sea. Spawning is always in the spring, when the water temperature is in the mid-fifty- to sixty-degree range. The females average four to five pounds, although six to seven pounds is common, and they can be as much as thirty inches in length. Males are smaller.

In the Delaware River, adult shad swim up as far as northeast Pennsylvania. The Lenapes observed the shad traveling in very large numbers; they are school fish, as are all in the herring family. The Native Americans had several methods of trapping shad, taking advantage of their characteristics—the fact that they ran dependably in the Delaware and its tributaries every spring, that the adults were seeking food on the downriver run and that they moved together in huge groups.[5]

The Lenapes used various types of weirs—obstructions placed in a tidal flow that direct fish into a pen designed to be difficult to escape. Shad were then easily speared. Nets were woven from tall grasses; bow and arrows, hand poles and scoop nets also were used to capture prey.[6]

The Native Americans maintained several large seasonal encampments: one between the Cohoquinoque and the Cohocksink Creeks, another camp located south of the Cohoquinoque at Wickquakonick/Wicaco, a third camp farther south at Passyunk and a major summer encampment at the mouth of the Cohocksink Creek. This latter village was called Kackamensi/Shackamaxon.[7]

This was the Lenni-Lenape migratory pattern until the first contact with Europeans.

Philadelphia region when it was known as Coaquannock. The Lenni-Lenapes had seasonal fishing camps from Shackamaxon to Passyunk. *Collection of the Historical Society of Pennsylvania.*

IN 1609, THE ENGLISH navigator Henry Hudson, seeking a passage through North America for the Dutch East India Company, documented the existence of another great bay north of the Chesapeake; this led to the Dutch establishing a claim. The Dutch incorporated the area of the Delaware Bay into the New Netherland colony.

The English initially arrived in 1610. They named the bay and river for Lord De la Warr, the first governor of the colony of Virginia.

Dutch Captain Hendricksen was the first to map the Delaware Bay, which he published in 1616.

Each of these explorers, as well as the companies that employed them and the empires for which they sailed, had observed the great wealth that Spain was acquiring from the New World. Merchants and adventurers sought support from European monarchs and attempted to convince the powerful to authorize expeditions.

The Netherlands chartered the Dutch West India Company in 1621. The company was given jurisdiction over Dutch participation in the Atlantic slave trade, Brazil, the Caribbean and North America. To stimulate settlement, the company offered riverfront land grants to anyone who could plant fifty settlers in four years. The company knew that permanent settlement was the best way to hold on to territories in the face of competition from the British and the French. Although the Dutch West India Company did establish a small trading post on Matinicunk (Burlington) Island in the Delaware River and defenses such as Fort Nassau in the current-day Gloucester, New Jersey area, neither they nor the English were in any hurry to explore or develop this territory.

The chancellor of Sweden was persuaded by a plan Peter Minuit presented, and Minuit was granted a trading company. Investors raised funds and a corporation was formed, the New Sweden Company, to start a colony. Two ships, the *Fagel Grip* and the *Kalmar Nyckel*, with a crew of Dutch and German sailors along with Swedish and Finnish soldiers, sailed in 1638 to the Delaware Bay. Upon landing in what is now Wilmington, they immediately constructed a fort and sent emissaries to meet with the Indigenous people to begin negotiations to purchase land.

This first group of men was also instructed to convert the Natives to Protestantism, gather beaver pelts, grow tobacco, raise silkworms and explore for valuable woods and minerals.

The Swedish colony worked out a treaty with Lenape chiefs for land around Fort Christina, named in honor of the queen of Sweden. From the Indian perspective, the tribes could give permission for the use of the land but not for its ownership; they did not intend to transfer all their rights to an area. That was an alien concept. The Europeans, on the other hand, expected exclusive treaties. The Lenapes thought that it would be to their advantage to negotiate with all parties.

At its peak, the Swedish colony numbered about four hundred men, women and children, while there were still four thousand Lenapes in the region.

The ship *Kalmar Nyckel*, which brought the initial Swedes, returned to its homeport and transported a second crew the next year to the colony called New Sweden.[8] A twenty-seven-year-old Swede, Peter Gunnarsson Rambo, was on board not as a soldier or a bound laborer—he was an independent wage earner. He had a three-year contract to work as a farmhand.

European settlers generally preferred to acquire the already cleared fields of the Lenapes. They built substantial structures and erected fences to protect their farms. Of course, the Native Americans contributed more than land to the early colonists. They shared their knowledge of agriculture and introduced the Swedes to such crops as corn, beans, squash and tobacco.

Peter Rambo began working for the New Sweden Company as a tobacco planter on the plantation just outside the fort. By 1644, he had become a freeman and three years later married Brita Matsdotter, a Finn.[9]

The Swedish colony began corn and wheat production, hunted and fished to supplement their diet and started construction of log dwellings. The colony grew to claim land on both sides of the Delaware River, but it received little support from Sweden. There was a lack of immediate profit, and as a result, the investors lost interest. Soldiers and servants deserted due to the difficult conditions—the scarcity of women, the lack of basic amenities and the impossibility of family life.

Because there were too few willing settlers, recruitment of Finns, Dutch and Germans began. Upon arrival, these people scattered and created farmsteads along the banks of the Delaware River and its tributaries, most densely at Upland.

In 1655, the Dutch besieged Fort Christina. They had again laid claim to the region and encouraged settlement with a small military presence. When the Swedes retaliated, Peter Stuyvesant sent seven ships from New Netherland to attack the colonists. Faced with this threat, New Sweden promptly surrendered the fort. The Swedish soldiers sailed away, but the settlers remained. Peter Rambo was among those who met with Stuyvesant's representatives. Later, he and fellow Swede Peter Larsson Cock were appointed magistrates of the Swedish court by the Dutch. Little changed for the Swede and Finn farmers who lived along the river's shores throughout the different colonial administrations.[10]

Events in the New World reflected upheaval in the British Isles and increasingly hostile relations between England and the Netherlands. Amid the English Civil War and the rise of Oliver Cromwell, the Dutch became the world's largest trader. When the English responded to this reality by enacting the Navigation Acts of 1650 and 1651, the trade war became a two-decade, on-and-off, full-scale military war between the two countries.

After Cromwell's death in 1658 and the subsequent restoration of the monarchy, Charles II continued to harass the Dutch. In 1664, he granted land in North America to his brother James, the Duke of York—"all land west of the Connecticut River to the east side of the De la Ware Bay." Charles then sent an army to conquer the territory. Peter Stuyvesant was enraged by this action but was forced to surrender New Netherland.

In 1664, the settlers along the Delaware River found that they were now under English jurisdiction. The British authorities gained the allegiance of the Swedish justices Cock and Rambo by reappointing them and providing them with substantial lands in Passyunk. The two Swedes were valued for their ability to interpret for the old settlers and the Lenapes in communications with the English.

Peter and Brita Rambo had acquired three hundred acres in Passyunk by 1669 and had raised four sons (Gunnar, John, Andreas and Peter) and two daughters (Gertrude and Katharine). Peter Cock acquired the most northerly farmstead of the New Sweden colonists. In 1664, he patented the Shackamaxon Tract from the New Amsterdam governor just before the English took control. Peter's son Lasse occupied the six hundred acres of land with his wife, Martha Ashman, and their children.[11]

At the time William Penn was petitioning King Charles II for land in America, the Lenapes regularly sold their crops to the colonists, trading fur pelts, selling crafts such as baskets and, of course, treating for plots of land. By the late seventeenth century, Natives of both the Delaware and the Susquehanna watersheds relied on trade with Europeans for clothing, tools and weapons.[12]

John Kinsey, an English Quaker, and his daughter Elizabeth sailed up the Delaware Bay in 1677. Their destination was Burlington; Kinsey had been sent by the proprietors of West New Jersey to purchase land from the Lenapes for their trading company. Kinsey was ill, however. In a brief visit to the Swedish settlement of Shackamaxon before the final leg upriver, he arranged to purchase land from Lasse Cock, afterward dying en route to

Thomas Holme map of 1681. The properties of Rambo, John Bowyer and Fairman were along Gunners Run, which later became Aramingo Creek. *Library of Congress.*

the New Jersey settlement. After her father's burial in Burlington, Elizabeth returned to complete the purchase with Cock and signed a deed with four Lenapes for Petty's Island. The Native Americans had sold the land to Gunnar Rambo as well; he released his claim to it on the document. A few years later, Elizabeth Kinsey married a Burlington surveyor named Thomas Fairman, and they took up residence in Shackamaxon.[13]

William Penn succeeded in his application for a land grant from Charles II in 1681. Penn sent his cousin William Markham to the newly acquired forty-five-thousand-square-mile territory to act as deputy governor and to facilitate the transition of the colony. Thomas Holme was chosen to be the surveyor general of Penn's land.

Since Thomas Fairman and his wife owned land within Penn's purchase, he became acquainted with Holme and was hired to assist him with the work of surveying. Not only did Penn's officials rely on Fairman for his knowledge of the area, but Holme and Markham were also welcomed to stay at his home, Fairman's Mansion.[14]

Three of the largest landowners from the New Sweden colony—Lasse Cock, Gunnar Rambo and Sven Gunnarsson Svensson—owned land within Holmes's developing plan for the city of Philadelphia. The Cock and Rambo families sold portions of their property to Penn's representatives. Svensson had land in the old Lenape village of Wickquakonick, which the Swedes called Wicaco, now Southwark. He also sold some of this land to the proprietor.[15]

When Penn himself arrived in 1682, he was also welcomed to stay with Thomas Fairman and his wife. Penn's legendary Peace Treaty with the Lenapes was signed under the "Great Elm" on the grounds of Fairman's Mansion. With these negotiations complete, the city of Philadelphia was formed from the lands between the Schuylkill and Delaware Rivers. Shackamaxon became part of the northern "liberties" or unincorporated grounds north of the new city.

Chapter 2

SHIPBUILDING BEGINS

The first ships built in North America were constructed to replace wrecked vessels and for purposes of coastal exploration. Several colonial leaders sought shipwrights along with other skilled workmen for their settlements. This early demand for such laborers implies that shipbuilding, or at least the ability to accomplish repairs, was considered essential to the survival and prosperity of a colony.

Sailing vessels were built in New England at the beginning of the seventeenth century—on the Kennebec River as early as 1607, in New Amsterdam in 1615 and along the Mystic River in 1631. By the time the New Sweden colony was raising Fort Christina on the Delaware Bay, the West Indies trade had begun to interest New Englanders. There was a steadily increasing demand for larger ships able to make the long voyages.

By the 1670s, Massachusetts had developed a significant shipbuilding industry; its yards launched twenty ships per year. In the next decade, there were thirty-four shipyards in the northern colonies.[16]

Shipbuilding, or at least ship repair, was being done on the Delaware River as early as 1676. The high bluffs of the riverbank made it difficult to offload cargo except at Dock Street and at Vine Street. The English Quaker James West established the first large-scale shipyard at Vine Street several years before William Penn arrived. The shipwright constructed the *Amity* and was granted waterfront land in return.[17]

West had enough work to be able to acquire an adjoining lot in 1690, adding 40 feet to his 60 feet of frontage on Water Street. From Water Street,

Penny Pot Tavern. James West operated the first large-scale shipyard at Vine Street and owned the tavern. *Free Library of Philadelphia.*

West's lot ran 250 feet east to the river. He also owned the Penny Pot House, located on his property.

The work at West's shipyard was more repair than new construction. What new vessels the yard produced were small, as evidenced by the fact that seven workers could build one in a month. Some of West's employees boarded next door at his tavern, apparently receiving part of their wages in drink. Labor was costly—West spent three pounds on timber but thirty pounds for labor on one ship built in his yard.

In 1701, West accepted barter of beer, flour, butter, sugar and raisins in exchange for constructing a new sloop. This was equivalent to thirty-nine—the amount he charged for the work.

James West died in 1701. West's son Charles, who inherited the shipyard in 1702, continued to build vessels on the property.[18] Charles married Sarah Parsons, and they had three sons: James, Charles and Thomas.

Another Englishman, who came from a shipbuilding family in Bristol, emigrated as the elder West passed on. Bartholomew Penrose began working as a shipwright, and his sons and grandsons were the workforce behind the Penrose shipyard at the foot of High Street.[19] Joshua Humphreys apprenticed with the family.

Meanwhile, in Shackamaxon, Thomas Fairman was enjoying success. He was promoted to deputy surveyor of the Colony of Pennsylvania and was appointed to the first council. He built a larger brick residence in 1702.[20]

The new colony was growing quickly. When William Penn arrived, there were only a few hundred Swedes and Finns living in the lands that Fairman was surveying. Between 1682 and 1683, fifty to sixty ships docked at Philadelphia wharves. At the turn of the eighteenth century, there were 2,500 to 3,000 inhabitants in the new city.

John and Esther Bowyer voyaged to Penn's new English colony at about the same time as the proprietor himself. Bowyer was a shipwright, and it is likely that he was the first of this trade to settle in Shackamaxon. Soon after arriving, he bought sixty acres on land that fronted on Tumanaramingo Creek, called Gunners Run, from Gunnar Rambo in 1684. Since the creek was navigable, this purchase gave him access to the Delaware River. The couple lived on the creek until John Bowyer's death only four years later. They had had one child, named John after his father.

Esther then married Joseph Lynn, who was deceased by 1691. The marriage produced the second of four generations of Joseph Lynns. That year, she leased a piece of bank lot between High and Mulberry Streets on Water Street. Anyone in possession of a bank lot at that time was expected to construct and maintain a cartway and a wharf, as well as steps to allow access to the waterfront. John Bowyer was about twenty years old when his mother, Esther, completed this land deal; he must have built the required wharf, cartway and steps.

After her second husband's death, Esther married a third time to Josiah Elfreth. Their issue was a son, Jeremiah. Josiah had children from a previous marriage; one son, Henry, became a shipwright.

When young Joseph Lynn apprenticed as a shipwright to his half-brother John Bowyer, it was the beginning of the longest consecutive line of ship builders in Kensington.[21]

Chapter 3

ANTHONY PALMER AND HIS FIRST PURCHASERS

As the formation of Philadelphia progressed, three significant merchants sailed to Pennsylvania from the Caribbean. They saw opportunity in the area north of the growing city and began making land purchases in Shackamaxon.

Captain George Lillington bought four tracts of land between Gunners Run and the Delaware River from several Swedes in 1697 and 1699. Anthony Palmer joined his fellow Barbadian a few years later and started land speculating. Palmer purchased Lillington's 582 acres. Isaac Norris emigrated from Jamaica to Philadelphia and began to acquire land north of Palmer's holdings.

Palmer called his estate Hope Farm and resided there for twenty-five years. He expanded his land in 1717 and then again after Thomas Fairman's death, when he purchased property from Fairman's son and only heir, Benjamin. In 1729, Palmer sold Hope Farm to William Ball and with the profits bought Fairman's Mansion along with the adjoining 191 acres. Anthony Palmer renamed this northern half of the old Shackamaxon tract to Kensington.

Palmer took up residence in the old Fairman mansion and began laying out and naming the grid of streets on his land.[22] The lower boundary became Hanover Street. He christened cross streets King Street, Queen Street, Prince Street, Duke Street, Bishop Street and Crown Street. To the north, the divide between Palmer's lands and Isaac Norris's plantations was Norris Street. The old Frankford Road was Palmer's western boundary.

Joseph Lynn completed his apprenticeship and began a business near Charles West's shipyard. He acquired property in 1717—a bank and water lot between Vine and Callowhill Streets, beyond the Penny Pot House at Vine. Lynn built a pier and called it Langston's Wharf for Thomas Langston, the original owner of the lot.

In 1728, he bought two lots to the west, toward Second Street. Apparently, his shipbuilding business was successful; three years later, he invested, along with four other men, in the Philadelphia-built fifty-ton ship *Dragon*. Joseph Lynn may have built it. Eight years later, Lynn bought a bank lot at Front Street between Mulberry and Sassafras Streets from Thomas Penrose, a Southwark shipwright.[23]

James Parrock was a neighboring shipwright; he operated a yard at Sassafras Street. Parrock built the galleys (riverboats propelled by oars) *Greyhound* in 1711 and the *Mary* in 1712, as well as the brigantine *Rachel* the following year.[24] Isaac Norris ordered a sloop from the shipbuilder in 1724. Norris was adding to the five or six ships he already owned in whole or in part; the new one was christened *Bonavista*.[25]

Shipwrights like Parrock, Charles West and Joseph Lynn were increasingly being hemmed in by the growing port of Philadelphia, which was expanding its warehouses and controlling more wharves. Some craftsmen looked to Southwark to relocate, while others saw the advantages of the wide sloping beaches in Kensington, better suited to hull construction and spar work.

Palmer subdivided his Kensington property into affordably priced lots. Two singular populations were attracted to this offer in the relatively less developed northern "liberties." Their descendants would configure the waterfront for the next 150 years.

Shipwrights, mainly English and Welsh, composed the larger contingent. The men who worked in shipbuilding trades were clannish; they intermarried and kept business and craft secrets within the family. The remoteness of Kensington contributed to this insularity, and business and community connections began to develop that would define the neighborhood for generations.

The second group attracted by Palmer's land sales were "Palatines," German-speaking immigrants from the Middle Rhine region of the Holy Roman Empire. Part of the largest non-English-speaking migration to British North America before the Revolution, many of these people became fishermen. It was a simple enough job for immigrants, with little cost for equipment. Settling initially in the area around Gunners Run, these Palatines developed a livelihood centered on the massive shad runs up the Delaware River.[26]

All along the Delaware, fishermen operated fisheries in common for generations; the immigrants probably fell in step with the local tradition. Shares of the catch were distributed according to the amount of waterfront access or the size of fishing pier a family held. Fishing families spent winter nights hand-braiding nets, which they knit together when the busy spring shad season approached. For two or three months during the spring run, they fished from the shore with large seine nets, each requiring five to seven men to handle.[27]

It took these two groups a few generations to blend among themselves to form the core of colonial Kensington. Family networks, geographic isolation and marriage within the community added to the distinctness of the area.[28]

The southern section of Thomas Fairman's lands, which lay below Palmer's Kensington, was acquired by Thomas Masters, who purchased about one thousand acres. This included the area below Frankford Road but north and east of the Cohocksink Creek to the Delaware River—a neighborhood known as Point Pleasant. Point No Point Road led from there to Kensington.

As Penn had his First Purchasers of land, so did Palmer. Among these men were Charles West, John Norris and Palatines like Johan Georg Reiss and John Baker. The names of these Purchasers can be seen on the 1750 survey map *A Plan of Property in Kensington* [relative to Palmer Estate] *by L. Evans.*"[29] This map was prepared at Palmer's death.

In 1743, Charles West bought a lot between Palmer and Cherry Streets from Anthony Palmer and built another shipyard in Kensington. Charles achieved renown as a shipwright with his construction of vessels of 150 tons.

Charles West also purchased a lot adjoining Gunners Run from Isaac Norris. With his success, he had a mansion constructed for his family and called it West Hill. Its foundations still survive under the front office of the former Penn Home at Belgrade and East Susquehanna Streets.

Charles's son James, born in 1721, learned the shipwright craft and went into business for himself at the Vine Street yard. James was contracted by John Reynell in 1747 to build a seventy-five-foot, two-hundred-ton ship for London merchant Elias Brand. This was the *Tetsworth.*[30] James married Mary Cooper of the Camden Cooper family in 1748.

Their surname having been anglicized from Boeckker, the Bakers came to the Delaware Valley in the Palatine German migration. George, Conrad

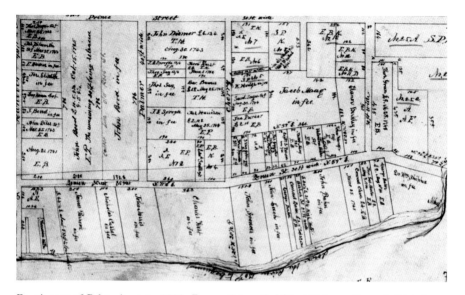

Evan's map of Palmer's estate, 1750. *From south to north, left to right*: James Parrock, Nicholas Cassel, John Norris, Charles West, John Spencer, Conrad Baker and Johan Georg Reiss. *Collection of the Historical Society of Pennsylvania.*

and John Baker purchased land from Palmer just before he passed away in 1749. Johan Georg Reiss, who also bought land from Palmer, had his name simplified to Rice. The Rice and Baker families were shad fishermen. Other early German-speaking settlers who joined the fishermen community were Cramp, Bennett, Faunce, Beideman and Tees.

Some families who were attracted to the sale of Palmer's lots were from across the Delaware River. When Gloucester was established in 1682, Thomas Norris and his wife, Rebecca, became early settlers. Norris was a farmer. Two of his four sons, James and John, became shipwrights.

John Norris moved to Kensington in 1737 to seek land from Palmer. He bought a lot on the newly laid-out Queen Street. The lot ran from Queen down to the river, at Palmer Street. A decade later, Norris and his wife, Sarah, subdivided their property and gave the southernmost portion to their daughter Rebecca and her husband, William Rice.[31]

Other First Purchasers of Anthony Palmer's land were James Parrock and fellow shipbuilders Nicholas Cassel and John Spencer. The lot Parrock purchased from Palmer was on the waterfront on the south side of Queen Street. Nicholas Cassel was a Quaker who married a woman from Burlington. He owned property north of Parrock's yard between Hanover and Palmer Streets.

John Ogborn, Richard and Henry Dennis and William Hayes were also pre-revolutionary Kensington shipwrights. Ogborn was from a Burlington family who had resided in West Jersey for two generations. William Hayes married Susanna, the widow of Benjamin Fairman, in 1742. Hayes worked as a manager of two inns, having acquired the Sign of the Swan tavern through marriage and operating the Sign of Three Crowns, as well as a shipwright.[32] Henry Dennis married one of Joseph Lynn's six daughters, Martha.

Many of these men had already been buying and selling land in partnerships and groups for a decade or more. In 1728, Joseph Lynn bought a house and a lot from James Parrock on the south side of Sassafras near Front Street in the city of Philadelphia. Richard and Henry Dennis made land deals in the Northern Liberties. Parrock and Jeremiah Elfreth worked on many land transactions together. They both owned a property along Point No Point Road in partnership with Joseph Oldman and Joseph Lynn. William Hayes and Samuel Hastings both made many lot purchases. James Parrock bought and sold more property than all other shipwrights. By the time of his death in 1759, he owned most of the land along Sassafras Street from Front to Third Streets.[33]

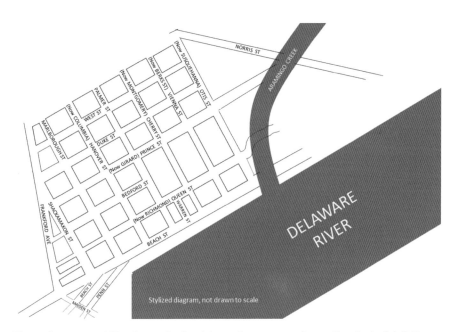

The major streets of Kensington in the eighteenth century and now. *Drawing by Bob Bell.*

Land, of course, was something concrete in which shipwrights could invest their profits, and it provided protection against the cyclical periods of unemployment in their trades.

Richard Wright, like John Ogborn, was a third-generation Burlington resident. Wright, Ogborn and the Shreeves (who later became known as the major rigging family in Kensington) were all Quakers who belonged to Chesterfield Monthly Meeting in New Jersey. Wright purchased land in 1743 from the Palmer First Purchaser Nicholas Cassel and then married Mary Coates.[34] His land acquisition at the foot of Palmer Street, and his marriage, led to the establishment of the great Kensington shipwright family of the eighteenth century, the Eyres.

When Palmer, the founder of Kensington, passed away in 1749, he left behind no male heirs. Although one of his two daughters married Alexander Allaire and a waterfront lot on Hanover Street was inherited by the couple, the balance of the estate had to be settled.[35] His property was surveyed (the previously mentioned survey by Evans), and many lots were sold to satisfy his debts. Palmer's will and the Evans map provide rare documentation of early shipwrights in the community.

Chapter 4

THE NORRIS, LYNN AND EYRE FAMILIES

During the War of Jenkins' Ear and King George's War, 1739–47, privateering in the Atlantic peaked. The American colonies supported Great Britain in its battles with Spain. Kensington shipwrights built ships for privateering and immigrant transport, as well as for trade. Philadelphia was one of the British army's main suppliers during these years, and the war trade stimulated expansion of the Port of Philadelphia. There was increasing demand for commercial space, and new warehouses sprouted at the foot of Vine and other streets to the south. This created growing pressure on the shipbuilders to relocate.

John Norris passed away at sixty-nine years of age in 1755. His sons John and Joseph continued to operate the yard at Palmer Street. Their brother-in-law, William Rice, was also a shipwright. He built a brig in 1757 that he christened the *Swift*.[36]

In 1746, Jeremiah Elfreth was working as a blacksmith. He bought a one-hundred-foot lot on the northeast side of Hanover Street in Kensington. As shipwrights began moving farther away from the city to enlarge their yards, men associated with shipbuilding were drawn along. Four years after Elfreth became a landowner in Kensington, his half-brother Joseph's son followed.

In October 1742, at fifty-one years of age, Joseph Lynn's health was failing. He had his will drawn up and divided his properties between his three sons—Joseph, John and Jeremiah—and three daughters. He died two days afterward.

The third-generation Joseph Lynn acquired land for a shipyard at Hanover Street. He purchased the lot in 1750 from Alexander Allaire. Joseph married Sarah Fairman, daughter of Benjamin Fairman.[37]

George Eyre, on a visit to America in 1727, met and married Mary Smith of Burlington. Among the five children of George and Mary were three brothers: Manuel, Jehu and Benjamin. When Mary passed away in 1750, George then married Rebecca Shreeve of another Burlington family. The Eyre patriarch and his wife were among the prosperous members of Burlington society, as was the shipbuilder Richard Wright. Eyre advanced his family's fortunes through the intermarriage of his sons with Wright's daughters.

The eldest son, Manuel, married Mary Wright in 1760. Shortly after their marriage, Manuel moved to Kensington, where he began work at the shipyard of his father-in-law.

George Eyre's second son, Jehu, followed his brother to Kensington and married Lydia Wright. When Richard Wright passed away, Manuel succeeded him in business. The two Eyre brothers began a partnership and built their first large vessel together, a barque named the *True Love*. Launched in 1764, it sailed for more than one hundred years. The third Eyre brother, Benjamin, later joined the partnership.[38]

Shipbuilding in Philadelphia had grown substantially since the days of James West. In the 1750s, shipwrights from Southwark to Kensington constructed 339 vessels and in the following decade built 240 wooden sailing ships of increasing size and tonnage.[39] By mid-century, Philadelphia had surpassed Boston as the major colonial shipbuilding center. The French and Indian War in 1754, concurrent with the Seven Years' War in Europe, brought increasing prosperity to the city. In one particularly productive year, 1765, 45 vessels were constructed along the Delaware River.[40] Blacksmiths, foundries, ropewalks and other associated industries began opening near the shipyards.

In 1756, England ordered the City of Philadelphia to house the new Royal American Regiment. British barracks were built near Third and Green Streets. Seven years later, Britain developed a defense plan for North America and thought it only fair that the colonists should help pay for it. Parliament passed three pieces of legislation designed to tax the British colonies in America: the Stamp Act of 1765, the Townsend Revenue Acts of 1767 and the Tea Act of 1773.

Americans reacted with a series of boycotts of English imports. When hostilities with the mother country occurred at Lexington and Concord in

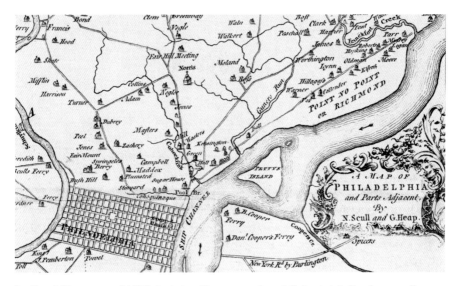

Scull and Heap map of 1750 depicting Coaquannock and Cohocksink Creeks, as well as Point No Point Road, which emanated from Point Pleasant. *Athenaeum of Philadelphia.*

the spring of 1775, each colony began to plan for its own defense. Eleven of the thirteen colonies organized state navies. Pennsylvania's State Assembly appointed a Committee of Safety, which considered how best to fortify and defend the Delaware River. The committee appointed a subcommittee for "construction of boats and machines" in July, and this body recommended employing Manuel Eyre and five other shipbuilders to construct galleys.

The Eyre brothers began their efforts by building the *Bulldog.* Gala ceremonies attended the launching at the Eyre shipyard, and the committee ordered all members to be present. Among the distinguished gentlemen aboard the vessel that day were Robert Morris, Benjamin Franklin, Anthony Wayne, Owen Biddle, John Cadwalader and Thomas Wharton.

Other commissions were given to the Eyres. They built two more gunboats: the *Franklin* and the *Congress.* Later in the year, in December 1775, Congress ordered thirteen more vessels. That was the birth of the Continental navy.

In December of the following year, the navy was ordered to support General Washington with his plan to move his troops across the Delaware to attack Trenton. Thirteen galleys transported men and material. Jehu Eyre, at the outbreak of the Revolution, organized his shipyard workers and his neighbors into a company of militia known as the "Kensington Artillery."

Among those from Kensington who pledged to defend their city were John Ogborn, John Sutton, John Cramp and men from the Baker family.[41]

Eyre was given the rank of colonel and was put in charge of the boats during the historic winter crossing in 1776. Jehu and his company then fought at Trenton and Princeton, later at Brandywine and Germantown, and then joined Washington at Valley Forge until January 1778, when the terms of his enlistment expired. Jehu Eyre served from 1775 to the end of 1777, all the while continuing shipyard operations to construct ships first for Pennsylvania and then for the Continental navy.

The Committee of Safety, which became the Council of Safety, in February 1777 created a navy board, and Manuel Eyre functioned as one of the board members. That same year, Manuel withdrew from shipbuilding; Jehu remained the head of the family shipyards in Kensington.

The third Eyre brother, Benjamin, served as lieutenant colonel with the Continental army from 1775 to 1781. During the action at Princeton, he was aide-de-camp to General Washington; participated in the battles at White Plains and Trenton; fought at Brandywine, Germantown, Monmouth; and wintered at Valley Forge.[42]

In September 1777, General Howe captured Philadelphia, and the Continental Congress evacuated the city. British officers commandeered the finest homes. A two-month campaign was then fought for control of shipping to feed the three-thousand-man occupying force, as well as the citizenry.

The Committee of Safety authorized construction of chevaux-de-frise (underwater obstructions) in the river below Philadelphia. The British realized that they would have to dismantle enough of the barrier for a ship to pass and disable the fortifications on each side of the river, while fending off attacks by the fifty-foot galleys of the Pennsylvania and Continental navies, to move upriver.

General Washington had hoped to hold the Delaware River until winter set in and the river froze over, but Howe requested reinforcements and got four thousand more soldiers. The American vessels exchanged fire with British sailors daily as the latter worked on opening a channel through the river defenses. Forts Mifflin and Mercer were shelled.

By mid-November, after a determined defense, all forts were lost, and the British ships successfully broke through the chevaux-de-frise. Most of the state and Continental vessels were destroyed.

During the occupation of Philadelphia that winter, tradesmen suffered from a scarcity of labor. It was very difficult for businesses—such as ironworks, sugarhouses and shipyards—to obtain supplies. The Kensington shipyards were burned by the Queen's Rangers, which also took retribution on the Eyre family by damaging Jehu's mansion on Beach Street. His family had relocated to Burlington for the duration of the war. British officers who quartered in the house through the winter tore up the elaborately carved wood paneling to use as fireplace fuel and burned the furniture as well.[43]

The British forces withdrew from Philadelphia in June 1778. Their navy, however, maintained a blockade of the lower Delaware River and Bay. Merchant ships clamored for protection. The Eyre shipyard was soon back to work building a privateer for a firm when the Council of Safety took notice and started negotiating with Benjamin Eyre for its purchase. The council's acquisition of the *General Greene* in March 1779 added a privateer to the state navy. Along with the Continental frigates, the *General Greene* is credited with opening the Delaware Bay to commercial shipping, to the great relief of Philadelphians.[44]

After the British departure, Jehu, Manuel and others purchased several boats and continued to harass the navy frigates in the lower Delaware. When the front lines of the war moved south, Jehu equipped several vessels as privateers. These ships sailed out to prey on Tory privateering vessels and to disrupt British commerce.[45]

Chapter 5

SHIPWRIGHTS BOWER, BRUSSTAR AND GRICE

STEAM TECHNOLOGY COMES TO AMERICA

After the cessation of arms were declared by both sides in 1783, the newly independent Confederation of States opened their ports to ships of all nations. Now that Americans were no longer restricted by the Navigation Acts, they could begin trade with such markets as India and China. But merchants' hopes for free trade around the world were overly optimistic. Britain did not want trade competition from its former colonies. Parliament issued an order in 1783 to block American vessels from the West Indies. In the Mediterranean, Britain refused to protect U.S. ships from the Barbary pirates. Merchants who had lost vessels and trading goods demanded the Confederation begin building a navy, but the individual states did not provide funds. It was not until pressure for protection grew much greater that a Constitutional Convention convened in 1788 to create a national government that could raise revenue and create a navy.

In Philadelphia, the end of the Revolutionary War initially brought an economic boom, quickly followed by a depression. Wages fell, and tradesmen were thrown out of work. Shipbuilding was hit especially hard. At the lowest point of the downturn in 1786, only a dozen ships were built at city shipyards.[46] A slow recovery began the following year.

William Bower, shipwright, was the son of Samuel and Maria Bauer of Southwark. William had served as a captain with the Philadelphia City Militia during the war. His younger brothers Joseph and Samuel also fought in the Revolution; they were assigned to the Sixth Pennsylvania Battalion. Samuel began his shipbuilding career constructing transport boats for troops. His first shipyard was at Maiden and Penn Streets in Point Pleasant. Early on, he and his brother Joseph and brother-in-law Morris Goff were partners. By 1789, Samuel had become the sole owner of the business. That year, he was selected to be a member of the Master Shipwright's Society.[47]

Samuel Brusstar relocated to Kensington from Southwark in 1771 and bought a waterfront lot. He was a lieutenant in the Fourth Philadelphia Battalion in 1776. After the Revolution, he bought land on the northeast side of Hanover Street between Queen and Prince Streets. Samuel's brothers lived nearby, Henry on Shackamaxon and James on Queen Street below Sarah Street. The family name was given to Brewster's Alley until Shackamaxon Street was opened from Beach to Queen Street. Henry and James were mast makers, complementing their shipwright brother's business. Brusstar's shipyard built the *Duce de Luzerne* in 1782.[48]

Francis Grice was from Naaman's Creek area in Delaware. He became acquainted with Philadelphian Richard Dennis, who offered to teach the young man the shipwright trade. Grice worked for Dennis until the Revolution began; he volunteered for the army under General Mifflin and, later, was a prisoner of war for three years. Upon his eventual release, he returned home to find significant property damage caused by the British during their occupation.

Francis's son Joseph also served in a Revolutionary militia, in the light infantry. He fought in the campaigns at Trenton and Princeton, returning home to assist the work on necessary ships for the war effort, such as the frigate *Effington*. Joseph joined the effort at the Eyre yards to complete construction on the privateer *General Greene*. Grice took work again with Benjamin Eyre in 1779 when the latter briefly partnered with Joseph Bower to produce the sloop *Mars*. At the end of 1780, Grice married Mary Smith and began his shipbuilding company in Point Pleasant. Joseph and Mary had many sons; among their issue were Francis, Joseph and Samuel.[49]

By 1785, innovations in ironmaking, coal mining, textile production and steam engines in England had been multiplying for a century. Denis Papin designed an atmospheric engine in 1690. It employed the vacuum created by steam condensation to let atmospheric pressure drive a piston. Thomas Savery responded to the need to drain water from coal mines with a steam pump. His engine also used the vacuum created by the condensation of steam within an iron cylinder, but the negative pressure in this case drew water into the chamber. Steam was then admitted to the cylinder, and it forced the water back out. The engine successfully cycled but didn't achieve much work.

Samuel Bower (1760–1834), one of the earlier Kensington shipwrights. Samuel's first shipyard was at Penn and Maiden Streets. *Mariner's Museum.*

Thomas Newcomen was inspired by the work of both men. Newcomen, an ironmonger, built a steam engine in 1712 that created a vacuum *and* drove a piston with atmospheric pressure. His was the first to convert steam energy into mechanical force using a horizontal beam. Later improvements would employ a crank to obtain rotational motion. Within three years, there were one hundred Newcomen engines pumping in England.

Scotsman James Watt increased the efficiency of the Newcomen engine by adding a separate condenser. He received a patent on his steam engine design in 1769 and, soon afterward, partnered with Matthew Bolton of Soho metal manufacturing in Birmingham. It was the world's largest factory in its time. Boulton & Watt engines soon began lifting water to turn the Soho waterwheels, draining mineshafts in Cornwall and, by creating rotary motion, driving a flourmill in 1785.[50]

Americans traveled to England and France to learn more about steam engine technology, and the occasional British engineer with hands-on knowledge immmigrated to New York or Philadelphia. Word also spread through patents that the inventors applied for and the lectures they gave to scientific bodies, generating published articles. Men of ideas were excited at the possible applications of the British Industrial Revolution.

In Philadelphia, John Fitch and Oliver Evans were preparing to make their own important contributions to the development of steam power. To understand Fitch's experiments in modifying Boulton & Watt's stationary steam engine to use in steamboat propulsion, a description of steam boilers in use at that time is necessary.

Newcomen steam engines employed a low-pressure engine with a large boiler, typically a five-foot-diameter riveted dome that rested on a cylinder of iron. Due to their shape, these types of boilers were called "haystacks." When water was heated from below, the dome would act like a big teapot.

While Watt focused on improving the engine, he still used a haystack boiler, achieving only a moderate increase in pressure—the maximum remained at five to six pounds per square inch. Evans and Fitch would modify Watt's engine and steam boiler.

In the year of independence, young Oliver Evans, son of a Delaware farmer, was working in a textile shop. He observed a problem involving the hand brushes workers used in those years for carding, and he offered to provide a solution. Evans developed a device that could spit out three thousand wire teeth per minute. His next project was to improve the process of milling. Over seven years, Oliver invented five machines that, together, automated the production line.[51]

Connecticut-born John Fitch had various occupations, from potash manufacturer, armorer to the State of New Jersey, a sutler (person who sold supplies to soldiers) to Washington's army, land speculator in Kentucky and surveyor in Pennsylvania. He was also a tinkerer and inventor; in his travels, he began to conceive of methods of transportation on land and water by steam energy. He had noticed the expansive power of steam and had some ideas about its practical application. Fitch relocated to Bucks County and was already developing plans when a friend showed him a publication containing a description of Newcomen's engine. Fitch also became aware of the steamboat experiments of James Rumsey in Northern Virginia; the two would soon be in mad competition to determine which would become famous as the inventor of the steamboat.[52]

Fitch sought support from the American Philosophical Society. Founded by Benjamin Franklin for the purpose of "promoting useful knowledge," the organization encouraged America's economic independence by improving agriculture, manufacturing and transportation. In the eighteenth century, natural philosophy, or the study of nature, encompassed the study of science and technology. This scholarly society functioned as a national academy of science. The State of Pennsylvania, in acknowledgement of the importance of the body, granted it a charter and a portion of Independence Square on which to erect an office. The location of Philosophical Hall, adjacent to the center of government, also demonstrated the esteem with which the American Philosophical Society was held. Chiefs of staff, cabinet members and even presidents consulted the society.[53]

When John Fitch presented his designs and a small model to a meeting of the forum, however, his ideas were met with skepticism. He needed to demonstrate that his steamboat would work, but he couldn't do that without financial backing.

Fitch formed a small company of shareholders in 1786, found a man with mechanical skills, Henry Voigt, to work with him and moved to Philadelphia in spring of that year. The partners rented a workshop in Kensington near the shipyards and began building a steam engine. Neither man had ever seen one.

By early summer, Fitch and Voigt had tested a model engine but found that the one-inch-diameter cylinder was too small to drive a piston; they ordered a three-inch cylinder. As the means of propulsion, Fitch initially considered paddlewheels but instead trialed a chain of paddles, unsuccessfully, followed by a complicated system of six oars on each side of their boat moved by a crank.[54]

The following year, the pair ordered a forty-five-foot boat to be built by John Wilson.[55] They fitted the vessel out with their steam engine, a five-hundred-gallon boiler and, incredibly, a three-ton-brick furnace with which to heat the water for steam.[56] The Eyre brothers (John and Joseph Norris), Joseph Lynn, Samuel and Joseph Bower, the Brusstars and Joseph Grice likely observed Fitch and Voigt's repeated testing of steam engines and propulsion systems with puzzlement.

Fitch must have interacted with the shipwright community to some degree, since his workshop was situated amid the shipyards. Along with Wilson, he worked with the shipbuilders' blacksmith, Peter Brown.[57] One zwonders whether Fitch's work was a mere curiosity to the local craftsmen or a source of derision.

In the summer of 1787, delegates were meeting at the Constitutional Convention in Philadelphia. Fitch invited all to join him on board the *Perseverance* for a demonstration. A few delegates accepted, and others observed the vessel's performance from the banks of the Delaware.

In the intervening winter months, Fitch ordered a new sixty-foot ship, and Voigt worked on constructing a pipe boiler to replace the brick furnace and built another steam engine with a twelve-inch cylinder. The two changed the method of propulsion to four large paddles in the stern. The new *Perseverance* made it to Burlington, New Jersey, in three hours.[58]

Fitch's nemesis, Rumsey, had constructed a pipe boiler and published an article about it with a drawing and detailed description. Rumsey claimed to have invented it in 1785. The tubing was a series of blacksmith-forged tubes, two hundred feet long, two inches in diameter and curved into a shape like a 1940s house radiator.[59]

Chapter 6

END OF THE CENTURY

EARLY SHIPBUILDING PARTNERSHIPS

The ratification of the new Constitution was proceeding among the states in 1788, and by that summer, it seemed assured. Philadelphia planned to celebrate with the largest parade any state had held so far to honor the adoption of the Constitution. They called it the Grand Federal Procession, and the organizers envisioned representatives of the city's trades and professions marching through the streets. On the morning of July 4, five thousand people stepped off to begin the three-mile parade. Military units, which were a traditional part of such events in Europe, as well as diplomats and city officials, passed by the throngs of citizens who lined the streets. Horse-drawn floats and a Grand Federal Edifice thrilled the crowds.

The trades had impressive delegations. Demonstrating that shipbuilding was one of the major industries of the city, the most respected shipwrights of the day, John Norris and Francis Grice, led their contingent of three hundred mast makers, caulkers, sailmakers, rope makers, block makers, riggers and carpenters. Norris and Grice were followed by Manuel Eyre, who carried a flag depicting a ship under construction. Recalling the event in his memoir, organizer Francis Hopkinson listed Rice, Brusstar and Humphreys, the Southwark shipwright, as members of the shipbuilding trades procession and described that they all wore "badges in their hats representing a ship on the stocks and sprigs of white oak."[60]

Both the China trade and the threat of Barbary privateers stimulated Philadelphia shipbuilding. In the mid-eighteenth century, Europeans became obsessed with Chinese furnishings. Fashionable parlors in London, Paris and

Vienna displayed Chinese design in rugs and porcelain, even extending the style to their gardens. In China, all foreign trade was conducted at Canton, and the most important trade group was the East India Company. Before the Revolutionary War, almost all American trade with China was done by the company through Britain. Direct Chinese-American trade began in 1784 with the voyage of the *Empress of China*. Philadelphian Robert Morris partnered with two New York merchants to send the Baltimore-built ship to Asia. Upon the *Empress*'s return to New York, American merchants took notice when word got out that the voyage turned a great profit. Within five years of Morris's success, fifteen American ships were trading in China.[61]

The *Asia* was the first Philadelphia-built ship to sail to China and the first venture of Stephen Girard in that part of the world. West Indies trade had been his primary activity from 1789 to 1793, but from then onward, Girard's West Indies voyages were superseded by those to Asia, Europe and Latin America.

In 1795, Girard worked with Kensington shipyards on four ships: *Voltaire*, *Helvetius*, *Rousseau* and *Montesquieu*. Rich Remer believes that Stephen Girard always used old vessels, which were rebuilt. Sources credit Isaac White for the *Montesquieu* and Joseph Grice for the *North American*.[62] Hoyt wrote that White also built the *Helvetius*.[63] Shipbuilder's certificates show that the brother-in-law and early partner of William Bower, Morris Goff, built the *Good Friend*, while Isaac White constructed the brig *Modest*, both for Stephen Girard.[64] Between the years of 1798 and 1826, Girard-owned ships sailed nineteen times to Canton.

Isaac White was commissioned a captain in the Third Battalion, Light Infantry, during the Revolutionary War. His shipyard was at Joseph Bower's wharf. Isaac and Joseph's brother Samuel were also founders of the Second Baptist Church in Kensington.[65]

American merchants' success in this new market called for ships that were longer, larger and faster. Philadelphia shipwrights responded. In 1795, one yard built five ships for the China and India trade.[66]

Management of the Eyre shipyard fell to Jehu and, after Jehu's death in 1781, to his eldest son, George. After the Revolution, the youngest of the three original brothers, Benjamin, entered into commerce and was involved in the China trade. He also became a warden of the Port of Philadelphia before he passed away in 1789.[67]

Between 1793 and 1794, George Eyre constructed at least four vessels: two brigs, the *Democrat* and *Harmony*; one ship, the *Charlotte of Charleston*; and one brigantine, *Sea Nymph*.[68]

Good Friend, built by Morris Goff for Stephen Girard. *Free Library of Philadelphia.*

Manuel Eyre became increasingly involved in politics. He was a delegate to the Provincial Convention of 1775 and one of the members of the Pennsylvania Naval Board in 1777 and eventually became a justice for the Court of Common Pleas. He had to resign as a justice when he was elected in 1784 by the township of Northern Liberties to serve as its representative in the assembly.[69] Four shipbuilder certificates from 1793 and 1794 were signed by Manuel Eyre, who would have been fifty-seven years of age. On the certificate for the schooner *Betsy*, Manuel is also listed as the owner.[70] He lived until 1805. His son Manuel began a very successful mercantile partnership with Charles Massey in 1803.

In 1754, Elizabeth Norris, daughter of John and Sarah, sister to Joseph and John Norris (the master carpenter who was honored in the Federal Procession in 1788), married Griffith Vaughan. They had sons William, Thomas and Samuel.

Griffith lived in Mulberry Ward (Seventh to Front, Mulberry to Vine Streets) with his wife and children until 1781, when he moved his family to Kensington; he later died the same year. William and Thomas Vaughan apprenticed at their Norris uncles' shipyard at Palmer Street. Soon a woman from New Jersey, Mary Furnis, would become intertwined with the Vaughans, further cementing Kensington shipwright families.

Henry Van Hook lived near the Maurice River in South Jersey; he acquired land and a sawmill. In 1784, he took Mary Furnis as his wife. The issue of their marriage was a son, William, and two daughters, Roxanna and Margaret. When Henry passed away in 1806, Mary moved to Southwark. Her second marriage was to William Vaughan, who was at that time a widower and a Kensington ship carpenter.

William Vaughan's brother Thomas married and had a son, also named Thomas. Brothers William and Thomas did not continue long in the shipbuilding trades; both became grocers. William Vaughan used his wife's inheritance from her first husband's New Jersey sawmill to get established. Once Thomas Vaughan Jr. completed his apprenticeship at the family shipyard, he became a successful shipwright, partnering with Samuel Bower in 1800.[71]

Since independence, American merchant ships sailing the Atlantic had been threatened with capture by the Barbary pirates. Additionally, the 1789 French Revolution would lead to years of ship and cargo seizure by both French and British ships.

During his second term in office, George Washington issued a Proclamation of Neutrality, which the French and British found a legal basis to ignore. It was obvious that the new country's trade needed protection. Congress in 1793 began debating whether to create an American navy. Six frigates were authorized the next year, each to be built in a different American port. Joshua Humphreys was awarded the contract for the *United States*, one of the six ships. Humphreys moved his shipyard the following year to a location near Old Swedes Church in Southwark where Federal Street now meets the Delaware River.

During the last three years of the eighteenth century, the United States conducted a quasi-war with France. French privateers succeeded in capturing three hundred ships.[72]

Despite these challenges to shipping, American commerce flourished. Historian Richard Miller observed that "the wars of the French Revolution brought an increased European demand for American farm produce and a rise in prices for it."[73]

As the Napoleonic Wars evolved, the French blockaded British ports, causing Great Britain to respond with a blockade of French ports. The neutral American ships became the carriers for world trade. The number of shipyards and piers in Kensington doubled during the first decade of the nineteenth century.[74]

John Norris Jr. died in 1792. In his will, he left to his wife, Mary, his brick house and lot situated on Queen Street. Norris's will also mentioned ownership of his wharf. Thomas Vaughan Jr. signed as a witness. In describing the borders of the Norris property, the document states that the Cramp lot was on one side. John Norris Jr.'s two sons, Thomas and Joseph, labored for years as shipwrights at the Norris yard at Palmer Street.[75] Thomas Norris built the brig *Ann* in 1793 and, the next year, the brig *Nancy* with Joseph.[76]

John Jr.'s brother Joseph Norris retired from the family shipyards at sixty-seven years of age in 1797. He lived out the next twenty-eight years of his life as a gentleman in the city, residing at 140 Chestnut Street. Joseph Lynn similarly left the trades and became a gentleman living at 5 Chancery Lane in the years 1797 to 1801.

Another of this generation to retire was Samuel Brusstar in 1794. His son Samuel worked as a shipwright, but he died at thirty-three years of age. The third-generation shipbuilder, Samuel's grandson Samuel B., carried on the family tradition.

Samuel Bower built the *Indostan* for the East Indies trade in 1795 and, the following year, launched the *Sam Smith*. Shipwright certificates attributed to Samuel's brother Joseph are evidence of his construction of two brigs and two ships in 1793 and 1794.[77]

Chapter 7

FITCH AND EVANS

After much discussion by Congress, the federal government passed the first patent law in 1790. John Fitch and Oliver Evans both applied for patents immediately. In Evans case, the patent design he drew was for his automatic mill. When granted, his was the third patent ever to be issued in America. Within two years, Evans had licensed his technology to more than one hundred mills.

The young man had more ideas to implement when he moved his family to Philadelphia. He built a blacksmith shop and set up an ironworks that made parts for mills that used his components. Oliver opened a store at Ninth and Market where orders for such parts could be placed.[78]

John Fitch's experience with the new patent law was far more problematic. Three other men applied for steamboat engine patents that spring, just as he did, and Fitch was furious. He and James Rumsey, who held one of the competing patents, had been conducting a very public pamphlet war in which each argued for the superiority of their designs. Nathan Read from Massachusetts and John Stevens of Hoboken were aware of Fitch and Rumsey's progress from reading their publications. Read had designed a tubular boiler, but instead of a single long bent tube (Rumsey) that exposed the surface of sixty square feet to fire, he drew seventy-eight single tubes grouped vertically, exposing two hundred square feet of surface to heat.

Stevens's steam engine design included an eight-inch-diameter, four-inch-long casing, but it was not a reciprocating engine. Instead of a piston, he fashioned a form of spinning wings inside. He employed a primitive screw propeller as propulsion. When he finally put together his steamboat in 1802, his twenty-five-foot flat-bottomed vessel achieved four miles per hour. Stevens's boiler was similar to that of Nathan Read's design, a tubular type. Functionally, many copper tubes, each one inch in diameter, conducted water through a fire-heated chamber to create steam.[79]

Fire-tube boilers became common, consisting of a tank of water heated internally by pipes funneling hot gases through it. Although their use continued into the mid-twentieth century, concerns about the pressure within the tank had engineers eventually realize that water-tube boilers were safer because they held less water.

Patents were granted to all four steam engine applicants. Fitch's dream of being credited with the invention of the steamboat was dashed—but not because of the patent confusion. Rumsey passed away two years later, and Fitch died in 1798 after years of disappointment. Robert Fulton, initially an art student in Paris, was lured away from the art world by his obsessive interest in European steamboat trials. Fulton returned to America and wrote a letter to Bolton & Watt ordering a twenty-five-horsepower engine, to be shipped to New York. In the winter of 1806, he hired a boat builder, craftsmen and laborers to assemble his vessel; the maiden voyage of the *North River Steamboat* occurred on the Hudson River the following summer.

Fulton's success was the result of several advantages: he had a wealthy partner, he acquired a ready-made steam engine and he was able to examine the work of other steamboat builders, including Fitch and Rumsey, as well as the now dozen U.S. steam power–related patents that preceded his efforts.[80]

Both Fitch and Fulton employed low-pressure steam and were only able to achieve speeds of four to five miles per hour. In 1803, Oliver Evans turned his attention to designing a high-pressure steam engine. He displayed his first machine to the public at his shop. Evans was able to use a smaller cylinder (six inches in diameter and eighteen inches long) than the low-pressure engines used at the Philadelphia Water Works, for example (a diameter of thirty-two inches by six feet in length).

To simplify, in Watt's engine, the work required to move a piston was divided between the force of steam pressure pushing in one direction and then the negative force of a vacuum created by condensation pulling in the opposite direction. Evans's major design change was to use high-pressure steam to achieve all the work of pushing the piston. His engines were simpler and less costly to make than condensing engines.

He received a commission from the City Board of Health to provide a dredger to be used to keep a proper depth around the docks. The Orukter

Amphibolos had a high-pressure steam engine and moved under its own power. It had to have small components to be mobile. Evans drove his bizarre invention up Market Street and into the Schuylkill River, where it did not quite perform up to the expectations of the city.

Over the next six years, he founded and organized Mars Works in Philadelphia with the intent to build boilers and steam engines. There were only a handful of working steam engines in the country at that time and even fewer workshops with the knowledge of how to build them. Mars Works had a pattern shop, an iron foundry and a smithy. Oliver's steam engines operated at pressures greater than fifteen to twenty pounds per square inch.

By 1811, thirty-five men were employed by Mars Works. Evans built the Columbian engine; it consisted of a vertical cylinder that drove a crankshaft and a flywheel by using a working beam (referred to as "grasshopper straight-line linkage"). By 1820, many western steamboats were constructed with Columbian engines onboard.

Mars Works constructed more than one hundred steam engines for marine use and industrial power before burning to the ground in 1819. Evans, who had been suffering from lung inflammation for weeks, died four days after the fire.

Oliver Evans's steam engine patents expired in 1824. After that year, his designs were used widely, modified and improved. Low-pressure steam engines in factories and waterworks were replaced by high-pressure engines by the 1820s.[81] And Kensington shipwrights began to apply the local innovations in steam technology to their vessels.

Chapter 8

THE NINETEENTH CENTURY

KENSINGTON SHIPYARD EXPANSION

Philadelphia Germans primarily belonged to either Lutheran or Reformed congregations. The Lutherans built two churches: St. Michael's in 1748 and Zion in 1769. The congregations combined, and the new church was renamed St. Michael's and Zion. By 1806, some members desired to worship in English. Even though others rejected the change from German liturgy, St. John's Lutheran church, with services in English, was founded. Kensington Germans became more a part of the community when they switched churches.

As the Germans assimilated, the fisherman and shipwright families began to intermarry. The Beidemans were an example of German fishermen who married into the Kensington shipwright clans. Jacob Beideman owned a fishing wharf at the foot of Warren Street. His daughter Mary wedded the shipwright John Birely at St. John's Lutheran Church. John's sisters, Mary and Elizabeth, joined the Birelys to two other shipwright families: the Suttons and Millers.

Johan Georg Reiss, anglicized to Rice, also operated a fishing wharf, at the foot of Otis Street. He was one of Palmer's First Purchasers in the mid-eighteenth century. Of the five major fisherman families—Rice, Gosser, Cramp, Faunce and Bennett—the Rice clan had the largest contingent and, by the end of the nineteenth century, controlled the majority of shad fisheries. Inheriting Rice's wharf was his granddaughter Catherine, who married Martin Cramp in 1791 at St. Michael's and Zion Church. Their son William used the Rice wharf to start his shipbuilding career.[82]

The election of John Adams in 1797 continued the Federalist era for another four years. President Adams tried to maintain his predecessor's Proclamation of Neutrality, but the threat of a French invasion seemed real enough to get the public to support his proposal for defense. In the spring of 1798, Adams created the Department of the Navy, and Congress authorized new construction. By the end of 1800, fifty-four ships had been built by American shipyards.[83] In Philadelphia, navy ships were constructed at Humphrey's yards in Southwark.

The new navy cleared the home shores and Caribbean of French warships and privateers. This action in the Atlantic was concurrent with Nelson's victory in Egypt over the French navy. The French Directory subsequently decided that it had proven counterproductive to attack American merchantmen. The Quasi-War ended with a treaty signed in October 1800.

When Jefferson was inaugurated the following March, the capital was moved from Philadelphia to an undeveloped area that encompassed parts of Maryland and Virginia. He and his Republican Party had opposed the naval build-up and its associated expenditures. As a result, the new government ceased further construction.

A group of mercantile and manufacturing leaders formed the Pennsylvania Society for the Encouragement of Manufactures and the Useful Arts in Philadelphia in 1787 to strongly advocate for the development of American manufacturing. Tench Cox, in particular, encouraged southern planters to grow cotton. One of the society's first efforts was to build a cotton-spinning factory at Ninth and Market Streets. In 1805, the first large cotton mill in Pennsylvania was established on the Cohocksink Creek in Kensington. By 1816, it had become the largest of its kind in the country.[84] When Eli Whitney successfully resolved the problem of separating the seeds from cotton, production of the crop grew at an astonishing rate. British textile mills had sped up the processes of carding, spinning and weaving; this, in turn, created an increasing demand. Cotton from the American South was providing half of England's consumption by 1810.[85]

Just as the efforts of promotion were showing results, American exports completely stopped. President Jefferson and Congress imposed the Embargo Act of 1807 in reaction to French interference with trade and British impressment of sailors. All American ships were forbidden to sail to foreign ports, and the navy was to enforce the law. For fourteen months, merchants ignored the embargo, traded goods through Canada and complained bitterly. The sounds of the saw, the adze and the caulking mallet in local shipyards were stilled as ship construction ceased. Jefferson's embargo turned out to be a failure. He repealed it before leaving office in 1809. By slowing imports, the president's action was an inadvertent boon to local economies and domestic trade and in that way provided impetus to American manufacturing.

The maritime industry made a quick recovery, and the burgeoning Kensington shipyards in the years of the Napoleonic Wars encouraged the shipwrights to form partnerships.

John and Mary Norris's sons, Thomas and Joseph, continued in the trade for three more decades. George Eyre was active in his father and uncle's yards until 1808, and his brother Jehu produced vessels at the Eyre yard until 1833.

The only recorded vessel constructed by the short-lived partnership of Samuel Bower and Thomas Vaughan Jr. was the coastal trading ship the *Rebecca Sims* in 1801.[86] Bower, one of the Point Pleasant shipbuilders, expanded to a second yard in 1809 with the purchase of land 190 feet north of Maiden Street on the east side of Penn Street. During the first five years of the new shipyard, Samuel repaired or built fifty-five ships.[87]

When his sons became of age, Joseph Grice brought Francis, Joseph and Samuel to work at his Penn Street yards. The eldest, Francis, was eighteen in 1806. The brothers gained experience and soon received contracts of their own.

George Landell was another Point Pleasant shipwright. He apprenticed with William Preston and, at age twenty-one in 1808, became a partner of Isaac Eyre (unrelated to the Eyre brothers at Hanover Street) at his wharf near Penn and Maiden Streets. Stephen Girard was one of their first customers. Landell kept expanding and eventually owned five piers. He and Isaac Eyre were out of the trade by 1828, moving on to establish a lumberyard. Landell diversified further when he contributed to the founding of the Kensington National Bank.[88]

Isaac White and Samuel Bower worked together to raise the funds for and then build the Second Baptist Church. White continued to share operations at Joseph Bower's wharf, which was situated between Marlborough and Shackamaxon Streets. White was even more involved with the community as a member of the Kensington Fire Company. In the first decade of the new century, White had constructed, and was advertising for sale, the *Bordeaux Packet*, the *Ocean* and the *America*.[89]

Matthew Van Dusen was a blacksmith for the first twenty years of his life. He married Lydia Brehaut in Christ Church in 1783.[90] In 1798, Van Dusen purchased a waterfront lot from a shipwright named William Yard on the south side of Hanover Street—a portion of what had been the Fairman

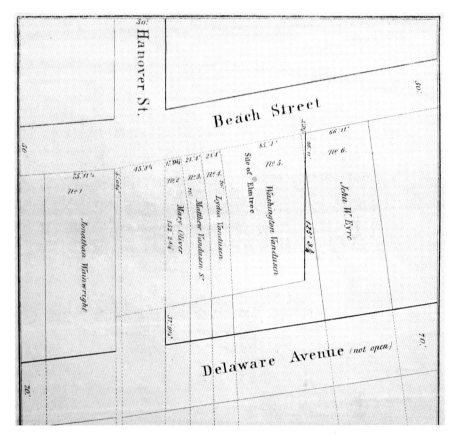

Van Dusen properties. Washington Van Dusen occupied the Fairman Mansion until 1820. Jehu W. Eyre oversaw the Eyre shipyard on the next lot. *Daniel M. Dailey Collection.*

property. Joseph Lynn possessed the historical land before 1765, and ownership passed to another man, Thomas Hopkins, and then to Joseph Ball before being sold to Yard.[91]

After he acquired this land, Van Dusen changed his means of livelihood and became a shipbuilder. He established a shipyard that he left to his sons upon his death in 1812. Operation of the yards fell to the eldest, Nicholas, the following year. His brothers Matthew and Washington began their employment in the family shipyard when they were old enough to apprentice.

The Vaughan and Van Hook families became further entwined when Thomas Vaughan Jr. married Margaret, Henry Van Hook and Mary Furnis's daughter. As was the case with Mary Furnis, the death of a spouse would mean remarriage, occasionally more than once. Complicating the Vaughan dynasty was the fact that Thomas Jr.'s father had been married a second time and that two sons of that marriage, John and William B. Vaughan, entered the shipwright trades.

John Vaughan apprenticed with his stepbrother, Thomas. William B. Vaughan and Roxanna, Margaret Van Hook's sister, married in 1812 at Kensington Methodist Episcopal Church. The shipwright brother of the Van Hook sisters, William, lived nearby on Beach Street near Hanover Street.[92]

Chapter 9

THE WAR OF 1812 AND A CHANGE OF FOCUS FOR PHILADELPHIA

The continuing British impressment of American sailors was one of the major issues that led an infuriated Congress to declare war in 1812. Parliament, however, was more concerned with Napoleon than with the U.S. Navy. The British merchant fleet considered American privateers to be an increasingly costly problem. More than five hundred of these privately armed vessels prowled the seas wherever British traders could be found, from the North and South Atlantic to the Far East.[93] When the British navy succeeded in blockading the coastline and took control of the Delaware Bay, another blow was dealt to the Kensington shipbuilding industry.

Congress had authorized four seventy-four-gun "sails of the line," the largest class of warship of that era, and six frigates in late 1812. The USS *Guerriere* was the first of the frigates to be constructed. It was built at the Philadelphia Navy Yard under the supervision of brothers Joseph and Francis Grice and launched in June 1814.

When the French were finally defeated at Leipzig, the British navy's need for sailors diminished, impressment ceased and Madison negotiated for peace at the end of 1814. With Napoleon in exile and Parliament now formally recognizing American shipping rights, British and French interference with naval and merchant vessels ended. The Barbary States, though, continued to capture ships and crews. The U.S. Navy was sent to Algiers. Stephen Decatur led the first of two squadrons as captain of the new USS *Guerriere*. After Decatur's squadron defeated two Algerine warships, a lasting treaty was penned with each of the Barbary powers. For the first time since

Independence, American ships could sail the Atlantic and Mediterranean without harassment.

After the War of 1812, Philadelphia never regained the level of maritime trade it experienced before Jefferson's embargo. Dramatic changes were occurring to the U.S. economy. Capital, which had substantially invested in merchant shipping, was shifting away from commerce into industry. Americans were expanding domestic manufacturing and markets rather than looking to Europe for goods.

From this point onward, New York City took the lead in American merchant shipping. British textile manufacturers chose the New York market for dumping surplus cotton products. And a new idea was put into practice in 1818 by the New York Black Ball line: regularly scheduled transatlantic freight and passenger service to replace spring and fall sailings. The line operators publicized a departure from New York to Liverpool on a fixed day of the month irrespective of cargo or passengers. The service took several years to establish itself, and it was not until 1822 that the Black Ball increased sailings to two per month. These ship lines were referred to as "packets," referencing the packs of mail that were carried aboard. Packets contracted with governments to transport mail, specie (currency in the form of coin) and official dispatches. Doerflinger described Philadelphia's economic changes as "a successful transition from maritime commerce to banking, manufacturing, mining and coastal trade."[94]

The Kensington shipbuilding trades, along with the rest of the city, suffered through an economic panic in 1814 followed by a severe depression from 1819 to 1820. Brewington wrote that just as it seemed Philadelphia shipwrights were at their most destitute, "the tide turned, and our shipbuilding began a new era."[95]

Thomas P. Cope was a Philadelphia merchant who had diverse business interests; shipping was but one of those. He and two partners commissioned George Eyre's brother Franklin to construct the *Susquehanna* in 1806. This ship, and the *Lancaster* in 1811, made many voyages to Calcutta and Canton.

Cope established the first Philadelphia packet line to Liverpool in 1821. It also provided regularly scheduled service.[96] Thomas partnered with his son Henry under the name Thomas P. Cope & Son. The firm had three more ships built for the packet line by Robert Burton; the only historical mention of him exists in the Cope family papers.[97]

Soon after John Vaughan completed his apprenticeship with his stepbrother Thomas Jr., he established his own shipyard at Shackamaxon Street in 1810. This member of the Vaughan clan would prove to be one

John Vaughan and Samuel Bower constructed an early paddlewheel steamship, the *Philadelphia*, in 1816. *Daniel M. Dailey Collection.*

of the most innovative and productive of the Kensington shipwrights of his day. He is credited with introducing black larch wood for use as "knees" (L-shaped braces inside the hull) of vessels.[98] Such densely grained wood provided the tensile strength needed when navigating the rough Atlantic.

John formed Vaughan & Bower to start constructing the first steam-powered vessels, launching the *Baltimore* at the end of 1815.[99] Starting in 1816, Bower built several steamships for use on coastal rivers.[100]

In these years of the existence of Oliver Evans's Mars Works, there was another mechanic who began collaborating with the Kensington shipyards. Daniel Large had a steam engine manufacturing company on Front Street above Germantown Road. In 1812, he and Francis Grice applied for a steamboat patent. The same year, Large provided a steam engine for Joseph and Francis Grice's *Delaware.*[101]

Joseph Grice moved to Virginia, where his sons joined him in his efforts to acquire large quantities of timber for the government. One of the Grice brothers, Joseph, contracted an illness on this mission and died.[102] Francis relocated to Norfolk and went on to fame as the government's naval constructor at the Gosport Naval Yard. Samuel returned to Philadelphia and continued operations at the family shipyard in Point Pleasant.

At this point in Kensington maritime history, formation of partnerships accelerated, and shipwright families expanded their original property holdings.

Jacob Tees was active as a shipwright from 1818 to mid-century. In April 1822 the firm of Tees, Van Hook, Bower & Van Dusen launched a 330-ton ship for the London trade, and another 400-ton vessel was prepared as a Liverpool packet. The next year, Thomas Vaughan Jr. and his brother-in-law William Van Hook bought a lot on the southeast corner of Queen and Marlborough Streets. Bower & Van Dusen launched an 1,800-ton vessel in 1825.

Elizabeth and William Van Hook acquired a lot, extending to the Delaware River, at Allen and Beach Streets during these same years. In 1826, Van Hook sold his steam sawmill and the ground it stood on to Jacob Tees. The next year, Tees and Van Hook along with Matthew Van Dusen and Joshua Bower, Joseph's son, constructed a large ship capable of carrying sixty guns, for the foreign market. When it was completed, Scharff and Wescott described the celebratory event: "Several companies of militia were on board when she was launched and 20,000 people were spectators."

Jacob Tees partnered with Samuel Tees in 1829 to build ships. This firm lasted six years.

Thomas Vaughan Jr. and John Vaughan expanded their holdings. Both were listed as principals for the wharf and shipyard below the foot of Marlborough Street.[103]

Blacksmith Michael Lynn and his wife, Susanna, lived on Beach Street near Hanover; Michael plied his trade in this Kensington neighborhood until 1813. Their sons, Robert and John F., were respectively a shipwright and a ship joiner, both residing at addresses on Beach Street.

Brewington stated that besides the Cope Line, there were "twenty-three other lines which ran from Philadelphia to all the Atlantic and Gulf ports." He went on to say that the vessels used in these packet lines—built by the Vaughans, Lynns and Van Dusens—"originated a new model which was eventually adopted as the standard for the famous New York Black Ballers."[104]

Chapter 10

THE BEGINNINGS OF CRAMP AND
THE RISE OF THE RAILROAD

The first vessel built by William Cramp was a sloop christened *Elizabeth* and built in 1829 at the Otis Street shipyard.[105] The Otis Street yard had been John Georg Rice's shad fishing wharf that his granddaughter, Catherine, William Cramp's mother, had inherited. Farr and Bostick state that William's mentor was Samuel Grice.[106] John Birely, the uncle of his new wife, Sophia, was surely an important influence as well.

The mining of eastern Pennsylvania anthracite stimulated further development of stationary steam engines, which in turn increased demand for better-quality iron. These innovations, along with its own mechanical creativity, moved Philadelphia definitively from a simple adapter of the British Industrial Revolution to being the "Workshop of the World."

Of the four types of coal—lignite, subbituminous, bituminous and anthracite—the latter has been subjected to the most pressure and heat, making it the most compressed and hardest and containing the highest percentage of carbon. Blacksmiths in the city, since before the Revolutionary War, had been aware that the hard coal burned at a hotter temperature than bituminous coal. The domestic market resisted using it since it was difficult to ignite. By the 1790s, one thousand tons of coal were consumed annually, most of it imported from Scotland, Wales and Ireland.

Lehigh County entrepreneurs got their chance to sell domestic coal during the British blockade in the War of 1812. The coastal shutdown, combined with a firewood shortage, had eastern cities desperate for fuel. In the late summer of 1814, 150 tons of anthracite reached Philadelphia.

Jacob Cist of the Lehigh Coal Mine Company approached nail and wire works, foundries and steam producers, teaching them how to use the coal. When he found existing technology inadequate for igniting and burning anthracite, he drew up plans for new furnaces. Cist promoted Lehigh coal through advertisements in handbills and newspapers.

Josiah White and Erskine Hazard bought anthracite from the 1814 shipment to experiment with at their Schuylkill River rolling mill and wire factory. The two men had been using bituminous coal from Virginia for five years. White was so impressed with the new coal that he traveled to Cist's mine at Summit Hill and immediately negotiated its purchase. He also formed the Lehigh Navigation Company to transport it. The company's first shipment, in 1820, came down the Lehigh River to Philadelphia via the Delaware River. The following year, the mine and the coal barge firms were merged to create the Lehigh Coal & Navigation Company. White continued the effort to market anthracite and gradually succeeded in converting the public to its use.

After 1824, the coal market expanded rapidly. White and Hazard built a railroad in 1827 to speed transport of their product from mine to river. Miller and Sharpless wrote that it was probably the first commercially successful railroad in America. Three years later, at a second mine, they added a steam-controlled inclined plane to another rail line.[107]

With the expressed purpose of feeding the demand for coal, the Philadelphia & Reading Railroad was chartered in 1833. The company's plan was to connect the smaller lines to the rapidly industrializing Philadelphia region. Moncure Robinson became the chief engineer of the new railroad and was charged with directing construction of the line all the way to the Delaware River.

After spending some time in Philadelphia and considering the best locations for the P&R's passenger and freight lines, Robinson recommended to company managers that they acquire the Joseph Ball estate, one of the last waterfront tracts remaining vacant just north of Kensington. Ball's grandfather William had bought the property from Anthony Palmer and named his mansion Richmond Hall. A nearby village began to grow; it called itself Richmond. The company acted quickly on this advice.

Construction of the Richmond branch began in early 1839. By the summer, Robinson had ordered pilings to be sunk for the first five piers of the coal depot.[108] In January 1842, a train of the P&R departed Pottsville for Philadelphia, pulling seventy-five passenger cars carrying two thousand people and three bands from Pottsville. Upon arrival in Philadelphia, the passengers and musicians proceeded to parade down Market Street to a celebration where a chunk of coal dug from a mine that morning was symbolically burned.

Behind the first train that day ran a second, comprising fifty-two cars loaded with 180 tons of coal. By May of that year, trains were hauling coal directly to the Delaware River on the Richmond branch.[109]

Applications of steam power continued to advance. The low-pressure engines that were initially installed for the Philadelphia Waterworks pumps in the first years of the nineteenth century used enormous quantities of wood and frequently malfunctioned. When replaced by high-pressure engines, the pumps were then dependable and powerful, but even more fuel was needed.[110] Anthracite coal solved the problem and accelerated experimentation with steam engines and boilers at local foundries and machine shops.

Three key companies—the iron foundry, the machinist shop and the steam engine manufacturer—were forming at this time. These would develop into the industries that would work with shipbuilders to design new marine engines and means of propulsion.

Young Isaac P. Morris decided not to continue in the druggist profession, where he was briefly employed, and in 1828 left the business to join his brother and cousin in the iron foundry they had started. Together, they formed I.P. Morris & Company at Sixteenth and Market Streets.[111]

During the first few years of the Morris's new firm, an ex-seaman, inventor and businessman, Captain Richard F. Loper, settled in Philadelphia. He had created a line of packets that ran between Philadelphia, New York and Hartford. After establishing himself in the area and meeting local shipbuilders, Loper sensed the new developments in ship design and decided to change the vessels of his line from sail to steam power. He befriended Captain John Levy,[112] who would eventually develop a partnership with Jacob Neafie.

Neafie, of New York City, learned the blacksmith and machinist trades in 1831 at age sixteen. In a chance encounter in Barnegat, New Jersey, he met Thomas Holloway, a marine engineer from Kensington. Holloway happened to moor his steamboat in the bay. The Philadelphian offered Jacob an apprenticeship at his firm. While working for Holloway, the young man gained experience designing and building marine engines. After seven years, Neafie established his own shop.[113]

John Towne and Samuel V. Merrick established Merrick & Towne in 1835, and soon after, the partnership received a navy contract to construct side-wheel engines for steamships. Merrick was also interested in innovative

At the end of his career, Samuel Bower sold his shipyard to Thomas Coffin. Coffin, a Nantucket spermaceti merchant, constructed the Kensington Screw Dock on the site. *Independence Seaport Museum.*

Captain Levy, through his friendship with Richard Loper, was able to employ Loper's patented propeller at Neafie & Levy in the company's screw propulsion ships. *Daniel M. Dailey Collection.*

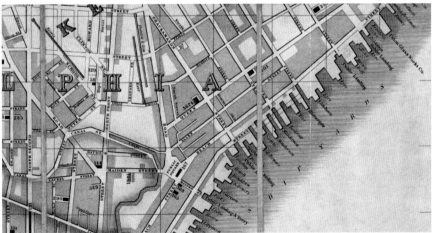

Tanner's map of 1830 includes the Beideman fishing wharf at the foot of Warren Street. John Birely came to own the pier when his wife inherited it from her father. *Library of Congress.*

ways to improve the lives of Philadelphians; he was instrumental in bringing gas lighting to the city, he cofounded the Franklin Institute of the State of Pennsylvania for the Promotion of the Mechanic Arts and he was among the group that founded the Pennsylvania Railroad. Samuel V. Merrick was the PRR's first president.

Samuel Bower continued to be an active shipbuilder until August 1830, when he sold his shipyard. He died four years later. The purchaser of Bower's property was Thomas M. Coffin; he erected the Kensington Screw Dock and Spermaceti Works on the site.[114] Samuel's nephew, Joshua, worked at the yard of his father, Joseph Bower, until 1833. It was situated between Marlborough and Shackamaxon Streets.

Chapter 11

TRANSITION YEARS AT KENSINGTON SHIPYARDS

Philadelphia underwent a rapid succession of events in the three decades from 1830 to 1860. Despite financial panics and depressions, the city's economy expanded tremendously throughout these years. One of the first traumas began with the election of Andrew Jackson in 1828 and ended in a major transition for the Kensington shipwright families.

The Second Bank of the United States in Philadelphia had a Congressional charter to act as the central bank for the federal government and, as such, was the depository of government funds. Nicholas Biddle, as the appointed executive of the Second Bank, held the power to regulate all other banks and enforce a standard of currency, which he determined to be paper money.

The president, in contrast, believed in hard currency and philosophically thought that banks favored wealthy easterners. At the beginning of Jackson's second term, he succeeded in ordering federal deposits removed from the Second Bank and placed in various state banks. Biddle lost the ability to control the lending practices of local banks, and easy credit with rampant speculation ensued. The national economy boomed until the winter of 1837, when the Second Bank of the United States was forced to suspend specie payments. Banks in New York, Boston and Baltimore followed suit, suspending payments. This abrupt change caused businesses to fail or to declare bankruptcy, banks to become insolvent and massive unemployment. The longest and most severe depression in U.S. history was underway.

For six years, Kensington shipyards endured slack work and periodic hard times. There was a reordering of shipbuilding companies as many of the small partnerships went out of business. It was almost a new cast of characters.

The Eyres ceased to be shipwrights; surviving family members Franklin and Jehu W. transitioned into the business of wharf building. John K. Hammitt would make a name for himself after the 1837 depression. Hammitt was a shipwright living on Beach Street in 1825. He married Hannah in 1834 and had a son named John H. The Birelys became more successful, as did William Cramp and his son Charles. The Van Dusens, Tees, Lynns and Vaughans were the other Kensington families who managed to stay in business.

Another epochal change was the transition from sail to steam power. Kensington shipyards had been building vessels propelled by paddlewheels and powered by steam since Vaughan & Bower launched the *Baltimore* in 1815. But paddle wheelers were not economical and became difficult to steer in heavy weather. Swedish inventor John Ericsson patented a direct drive design for screw propulsion in 1836. The design encompassed a longitudinal shaft attached to a propeller with four curved blades. This ensured better engine performance, increased maneuverability and mechanical efficiency and made larger ships possible.

Thomas Heinrich provided a fine description of the split that developed between the two major ship construction centers:

> *Shipbuilders were of two regional schools of thought regarding the merits of screw and paddlewheel propulsion: most New York builders used paddlewheels, Philadelphia yards opted for screw propulsion. One explanation for the preference of New Yorkers was the local demand for big steamships. Long hulls would have strained the propeller shafts. Philadelphia yards built smaller craft, such as river tugs and steamers for regional coastline trade. Even so, their larger vessels in the 1850s usually had paddlewheels. In Philadelphia, screw propeller construction was also a reflection of development in the engine building and tool making trades. In the first half of the nineteenth century, local Philadelphia shops developed strong demand for steam engines.*[115]

In 1841, the American navy asked Ericsson to design a small screw sloop, the USS *Princeton*. It was built at the Philadelphia Navy Yard, and its engines were cast by Merrick & Towne.

In the late eighteenth century, when the intermarriage of Kensington's fisherman and shipwright families began, the lines of three clans produced shipbuilders who would survive the economic turmoil and changes wrought by industrialization. John Birely lived a long life as a shipwright and builder. His sister Mary wedded William Sutton, who also had a very extended career in the shipyards and produced a large family of eleven children, including many sons who doubtless apprenticed with their father.

John and Mary Birely's sister, Elizabeth, married shipwright Henry Miller. Charles Cramp, in his biography by Buell, described Henry as having been involved in the China trade. He made four voyages to Asia before being captured by a French privateer on the return trip.[116] The legacy of his progeny was more significant. Henry Miller and Elizabeth were the parents of Sophia, who married William Cramp in 1827.[117]

As a teenager, John Birely served in the army during the War of 1812. He was commissioned a lieutenant. In the two decades after the war, John worked as a laborer and advanced to become a master shipwright. In 1816, fisherman Jacob Beideman died. The following year, John Birely married Jacob's daughter Mary and eventually founded the Birely shipyard at the foot of Warren Street, which had previously been the location of the Beideman fishing wharf.[118]

The ship *John Sargeant* was launched from John Vaughan's yard in 1831. In 1833, Jacob Keen Vaughan entered into partnership with his father. The two collaborated on the steamer *Pennsylvania*, designed to tow ships away from the breakwater.[119]

Thomas Cope turned over control of his shipping business to his sons Henry and Alfred, changing the company name to H&A Cope. The Cope Line, now Philadelphia's only packet, began to contract with John Vaughan & Son for new vessels. The first was the *Susquehanna*, then the *Saranak*.[120]

Jacob Tees's shipyard, as described by Rich Remer, located "at Marlborough Street, constructed nearly two hundred vessels during its operations from 1826 to 1857." His reputation was known around the world; the caliphate of the Ottoman empire extended an offer to Jacob to be its chief naval constructor (he declined). Tees married into the Norris family by wedding Francis Norris; their sons, Jacob and Joseph, were later employed as ship carpenters.[121]

Samuel Grice (1784–1849). Samuel apprenticed at his father Joseph's yard on Penn Street, later inheriting the business. *Mariner's Museum.*

The Norris brothers worked until the years of their passing, Thomas in 1841 at sixty-five years and Joseph in 1848, at eighty-two years of age. Joseph's obituary of October 11 in the *Public Ledger* of that year stated that his funeral was held in his residence at Queen Street above Palmer.[122]

Samuel Grice continued as a shipbuilder until 1837. In that year of economic tumult, and for the six years afterward, he worked as a ship carpenter. Throughout his career, Grice plied his trade at his shipyard at Penn and Maiden Streets, but in 1843 he became a lumber merchant, doing business at Beach and Hanover Streets, and moved his residence from Point Pleasant to Beach and Shackamaxon Streets—evidence, no doubt, of how disruptive the times were even to men with long-standing successful companies.

The effects of the Philadelphia industrial revolution on traditional shipbuilding men are demonstrated in the fortunes of the Van Dusen family. Matthew's shipwright brother John married a member of the Vaughan clan. Their brother Washington continued to reside in the Fairman Mansion until 1820. The mansion, even at that time, was a century-old relic of William Penn's day. Washington Van Dusen became known for his patent for the first marine railway in America in 1834.[123]

The same year his uncle received the railway patent, Nicholas's son, Joseph Ball Van Dusen, became employed by the Lehigh Coal & Navigation Company. He eventually operated the Black Diamond Colliery in Wilkes-Barre and became a successful coal merchant.[124] By 1849, Joseph was residing at 349 South Third Street and had established his business offices at Second Street near Market.

After the winter of 1836–37, the Philadelphia City Council established by ordinance the Trustees of Iceboats. Ice was an annual headache for shipping and commerce; action had to be taken to keep the Delaware River clear. The trustees, twelve citizens elected annually by council, had complete charge of construction and operation of the iceboats. The first contract was awarded to Van Dusen & Birely. The partnership launched the world's first steam-powered ice breaker, *City Ice Boat No. 1*, that summer. The vessel had paddlewheel propulsion and was also designed to be used as a tugboat. The trustees chose Matthias Baldwin, who had successfully trialed his first steam locomotive five years prior, to build the engines.

Subsequent maintenance of the iceboat in the next decade was done by many: Theodore Birely was reimbursed for painting, Merrick & Towne performed engine and boiler work and John Vaughan & Son and the Reaney & Neafie Company did repairs.[125] Jacob Tees was contracted for *City Ice Boat no. 3*.[126]

Along with the technological advancement of steam engines came the dangers of pressurized steam and water. Engines and boilers were of variable quality, sometimes reused; some ship engineers were inexperienced, and operators were always trying to keep to a schedule. Manufacturing flaws and procedural shortcuts by steamboat pilots led to accidents.

Nationally, steamboat explosions were happening with greater frequency, frightening people with stories of death by maiming, burns and drowning. Citizens demanded that the government respond to mitigate the dangers. As a part of the 1838 Steamboat Act, which became law in July of that year, Congress passed a resolution requiring the Treasury Department to gather information on steam engines and steamboats in use in the country. Other details were requested: the date and name of who constructed the engines, the type of use, whether low or high pressure was employed, a description of any explosions and number of fatalities or injuries and the names of the steamboat owners, captains and engineers.

The Philadelphia Customs District, as in other districts, collected the facts and responded to the treasury. The resultant report of the secretary of the treasury to Congress at the end of the year showed 260 accidents, all but 30 of which involved steamboats, and 99 of those were attributed to exploding boilers. All these malfunctions of the new steam technology led to an estimated two thousand lives lost.

Among the steam engine manufacturers listed were James T. Sutton and Thomas Holloway. Many Kensington steamboats named in the report were vessels from the yard of John Vaughan & Son. Other shipbuilding firms mentioned were those of Samuel Grice, Jacob Tees, Van Dusen & Birely and Tees & Van Hook.[127]

After the 1838 Steamboat law was enacted, accidents declined somewhat, but it was quickly realized that more effort was needed to enforce compliance. This had to wait for the subsequent 1852 Steamboat Act, which stiffened inspections; created standards for boiler construction, as well as rules regarding safety valves and operating pressures; and put in place a licensing system for steamboat pilots and engineers.

Chapter 12

THE SURVIVING SHIPWRIGHTS RECOVER

William Sutton's long career trajectory parallels that of the Eyres and Samuel Grice. Sutton started as a shipwright in 1803 and began building ships in 1813, and then in 1837, his status diminished as his recorded employment reverted to "shipwright." In 1842, his place of occupation changed to "lumber wharf," and finally, in 1848, he retired.

William Cramp gave his occupation as a ship carpenter in 1837 and his residence as Vienna above Queen Street. In the mid-1840s, he opened a second yard at Palmer Street. In 1845 and 1846, he was in partnership with Peter Cramp building boats at Beach below Palmer.

The depression stalled the young P&R Railroad Company's ability to access the capital it needed. But by 1842, it had succeeded in opening the entire line from anthracite country to the new terminal at Richmond on the Delaware River. Mine-to-ship transportation would now be possible, and coal would move directly to the Kensington foundries and machine shops, which had come to rely on the fuel.

An event that captured the attention of all American shipyards in 1838 was the transatlantic race between the British side-wheel steamship *Great Western* and the side-wheeler of a rival line, the British and American Steamship Navigation Company. The *Sirius* won. Two years later, the Canadian Samuel Cunard had a pair of paddlewheel steamships that provided regular service between Boston and Liverpool. The Cunard Line had the Atlantic to itself for ten years.

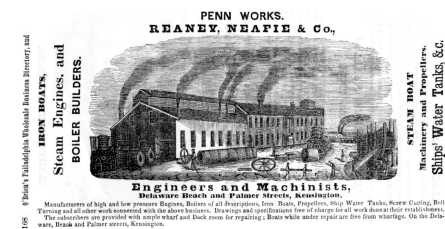

Reaney, Neafie and Company was founded in 1844 at Beach and Palmer Streets. *Free Library of Philadelphia.*

In 1844, Jacob Neafie and Thomas Reaney, along with John Levy, partnered to form the Penn Steam Engine & Boiler Works at the corner of Beach and Palmer Streets. The company specialized in steam engines and propellers for screw propulsion.[128] Penn Works obtained the rights to Captain Loper's propeller design through his relationship with Levy.[129]

Cramp's son Charles, born in 1828, served his apprenticeship with his great-uncle, John Birely. While Charles was working with him, Birely had been experimenting with Reaney, Neafie & Levy's marine engines. In a foreshadowing of his great career, as soon as his training was complete, Charles returned to his father's yard and immediately started work on a steam tugboat he called the *Sampson*—the nation's first screw-propelled tug. He also contracted with Reaney, Neafie & Levy for its engines. It was the beginning of many years of Charles's innovation with steam power and collaboration with the engine builders.

I.P. Morris & Company relocated as well, setting up at York Street, south of the Philadelphia & Reading Railroad's Port Richmond Terminal, to build and repair steamship engines and boilers.

William Cramp continued to build ships of wood despite the new technologies available. In 1906, Charles Cramp retrospectively commented on his fellow tradesmen by writing, "Most of these shipbuilders neglected to familiarize themselves with the application of the steam engine to ship construction even in the most general way and this resulted in a gradual elimination of the cult or guild of master builder."

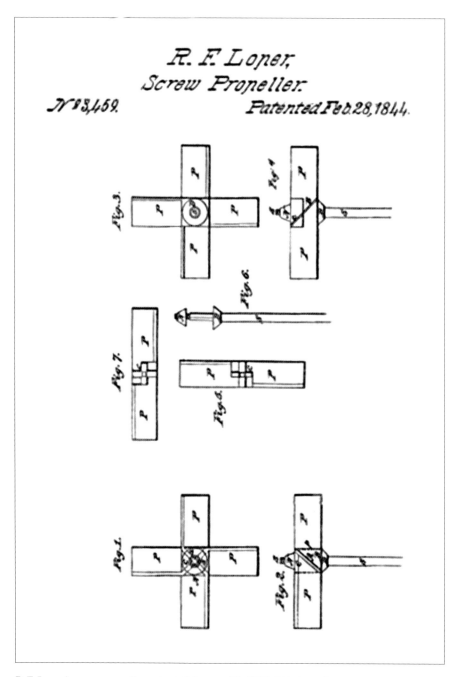

R.F. Loper's screw propeller patent, February 28, 1844. *Patents.google.com.*

Charles Cramp next built a side-wheel towboat, *Aspinwall*, in 1847 and two passenger steamers, the *Caroline* and *Albatross*, two years later. The company claimed that the former was the fastest propeller ship in the mid-Atlantic. William then turned his attention to clipper ships, such as the *Stillwell S. Bishop*.[130]

In the mid-nineteenth century and in the many years since, much has been written about the clipper ships of Donald McKay, Samuel Samuels's *Dreadnought*, Edward Collins and his Dramatic Line and races across the ocean in pursuit of the mythical Blue Riband. Shipbuilders and line operators in New York and Boston sought publicity to draw customers.

John Birely (circa 1797–1867), an early adapter of screw propulsion, influenced Charles Cramp. *Mariner's Museum.*

Each strove to claim the fastest crossing. Collins and Cunard competed for the first-class trade by offering luxurious accommodations and comfortable sailing.

William Cramp designed and built the same fast vessels, the only Kensington shipyard to do so. Clippers typically had three to four slightly raked masts, each mast holding five to six courses of sail. Their hulls had a narrow beam and a knifelike bow.

Two of John Birely's sons, Theodore and Jacob, had entered the family business by this time. Although it is not completely clear from sources, it seems that Theodore joined his father at the shipyard at Beach and Warren Streets, and Jacob went on to engage in a series of shipbuilding partnerships. Theodore was the older of the two, born in 1818. He had a strategic marriage. The wedding of Theodore and Sarah Loper, R.F. Loper's daughter, took place in 1838 at First Presbyterian Church of Kensington.[131] Soon after, Captain Loper began contracting significant business with the Birely shipyard.

The Mexican-American War began in the spring of 1846 after the United States annexed the Republic of Texas, which had declared its independence from Mexico. In the second year of hostilities, General Winfield Scott developed a plan for an army invasion of Mexico through the port city of Veracruz. Troops would be moved by ship and then landed using surf boats. The quartermaster received an order for 141 boats, each capable of carrying forty men. Captain Loper was hired as a special agent to acquire

Morning Light clipper, built by William Cramp in 1853. *Daniel M. Dailey Collection.*

such barges; he called on Birely shipbuilders to quickly construct all of the "lighters." Loper's goal was achieved within a remarkable thirty days.[132]

Jacob Birely was a partner at the firm Birely & Tees in 1851 at Beach and Hanover Streets; it lasted two years. He continued as a shipwright in this yard through the 1850s.

When John Vaughan died in 1846, the successors to John Vaughan & Son at the Shackamaxon Street wharf were Jacob Keen Vaughan and Matthew Lynn. This exemplifies the continuing succession of the Lynn family since Joseph, the first Lynn shipwright, founded his business at the foot of Vine Street in 1717. They had been among the original core of Philadelphia shipbuilders and had made connections with many other important shipwright clans over time, reinforcing the "family capitalism" basis of the craft. The Lynns would move from one joint venture, such as that with Jacob Keen Vaughan, to another with the Birelys. These were the older form of associations—informal and temporary mergers with other shipwrights, lasting only a few years. The new, more formal and permanent corporate structures were just beginning.

City directories show that John K. Hammitt started a business in the Point Pleasant neighborhood at Penn and Marsh Streets in 1844. There he constructed the *Dove*, *Tarter*, *Venezuela*, *Arrow* and the *General Paez*. Within two years, he was able to purchase Pier 43 at Maiden Street.[133]

Two Philadelphia firms were concurrently carrying on significant trade with Latin America. John F. Ohl and Sons operated in Havana markets, and Dallett Brothers' Red "D" Line maintained a route to La Guaira, Venezuela. This was one of the few ports in which Philadelphia enjoyed more trade than New York. John K. Hammitt was commissioned to build three barques for the Dalletts; one of the three was christened the *Thomas Dallett*.[134]

The Hammitt yards turned out many more vessels between 1846 and 1850, among them the *Isabelita Hyne* and the *Conrad*.[135]

A newly constructed John K. Hammitt ship was given a glowing report in the *Public Ledger* of July 1851. The newspaper described the launch of the *Shackamaxon* from the yards: "She glided from the ways in beautiful style, amid the cheers of the spectators, and as she gracefully swept out into the stream, the beauty of her lines and exquisite model challenged the admiration of all."[136]

In 1846, P&R engineer Richard Osborne expanded the Richmond Terminal to thirteen piers, making it the largest such facility in the Port of Philadelphia. John Tucker, P&R president, developed a system for unloading

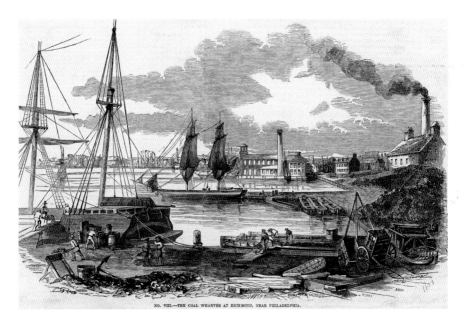

NO. VIII.—THE COAL WHARVES AT RICHMOND, NEAR PHILADELPHIA.

Coal wharves at Richmond. By 1842, the Philadelphia & Reading Railroad had succeeded in transporting coal from the Lehigh mines to the Delaware River. *Free Library of Philadelphia.*

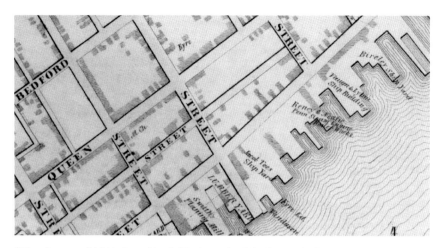

Sidney's map of 1849 shows Jacob Tees's yard at Marlborough, Reaney & Neafie and Vaughan & Lynn at Palmer Street and the Birely shipyard at Warren Street. *Historical Society of Frankford.*

coal from railroad cars into the holds of barges. The anthracite was then moved up the Delaware River, along the Delaware and Raritan Canal, and ultimately to New York and other northern ports. The railroad also added riverfront acreage and trackage under Tucker.[137]

Chapter 13

THE ZENITH OF WOODEN SHIPBUILDING AND IMMIGRATION PRESSURES

Heinrich wrote that the years from 1847 to 1857 "marked the golden age of American wooden shipbuilding." As he described, Birely & Son of Kensington constructed seven screw-steamers between 1849 and 1853.[138]

It is possible to account for seven steamers in that period, but from the evidence, two employed paddlewheels. When those were completed, the Birelys began installing screw propellers. The contract with Loper for the SS *Union*, one of the two side-wheel paddle steamers, was just three years after the work Birely & Son had done for the captain during the Mexican-American War. The *Union* was purchased by the People's Line of San Francisco and plied the route between that city and Panama until, after less than three months of service, it ran aground and was broken up by heavy surf.[139]

Others credit Theodore, or Theodore Birely & Son, for four of these steamers: the *Star of the South*, SS *Fremont*, SS *Arctic* and SS *Samuel S. Lewis*.

The SS *Fremont* was built by Theodore Birely in 1850. It was a side-wheel steamer with two decks and rigged masts for sail as backup. The original owners were the Pacific Mail Steamship Company. The company formed with the idea of transporting U.S. mail and agricultural products from the West Coast, but just as the line got its start, the gold rush began in the Sierra Nevada. The Pacific Mail became very successful, as its steamers moved many passengers and supplies to gold country. The SS *Fremont* initially ran between San Francisco and Panama and then worked the coastal service from San Francisco to the Columbia River.

The ubiquitous Captain R.F. Loper worked with Theodore Birely in 1851 to produce the SS *Samuel S. Lewis* for a Boston-Liverpool line. The steamer had a wooden hull, screw propulsion, three decks and three rigged masts and was 216 feet in length.[140] *Gleason's Pictorial Drawing-Room Companion*, a publication from Boston, had a sketch of the steamer that year with the following caption:

> *Our artist has sketched for us herewith the scene of the launching of the steam ship S.S. Lewis from the shipyard of Birely & Son, Kensington, Philadelphia. The wharves in the vicinity were thronged with spectators, attracted by the spectacle. The river in front was also covered with small boats, and shortly before the launch the steamboat Fashion brought up a load of spectators, and the Washington passing by from Tacony, with a band of music on board, saluted the new steamship by tapping her bell. At about a quarter of 1 o'clock, the beautifully modeled hull began to move along the ways, and the momentum accelerating her motion, she was soon gliding away gracefully upon the bosom of the Delaware, amid the shouts of thousands that witnessed the sight.[141]*

R.F. Loper and Theodore Birely collaborated on the SS *Samuel Lewis* in 1851. The sketch is from an article describing the launch of the steamer. *Independence Seaport Museum.*

The SS *Arctic* was a screw steamer that Theodore Birely constructed at the Navy Yard the same year as his work on the *Lewis*. It was another steamship with two decks, as well as rigged fore, main and mizzen masts. Reaney, Neafie & Levy manufactured the engine and tubular boiler. The *Arctic* was to be used as a lightship.[142]

The *Star of the South* was one of the first mechanically reliable and economically profitable screw propeller steamships. It was designed as a packet for a New York–New Orleans line, the Star Steamship Company. Brothers Thomas P. and J.W. Stanton owned and operated the firm, the former in New York and the latter in New Orleans. The Stantons commissioned Theodore Birely and Captain R.F. Loper for the hull and the propeller.[143]

Launched in 1853, the *Star of the South* could achieve 11.5 knots under steam power but was also rigged as a three-masted schooner. It made its first run from New Orleans to New York in eight days and then bested that time the following year by traveling the route in six days.[144]

Vaughan & Lynn launched an incredible number of vessels in the decade of their existence from 1847 to 1857. Their ships carried the largest tonnage of any Kensington yard. The partners built the steamships *Robert Burton*, *America* and *Ajax*. Their side-wheel steamers included the *State of Georgia*, *Keystone State* and *Quaker City* for the Philadelphia & Savannah Steam Navigation Company.[145]

The *Keystone State* was known to be a fast vessel on the route between the two cities. Its engine was manufactured by Merrick & Sons' Southwark Foundry. As were many side-wheelers in the 1850s, the paddlewheels were driven by a side-lever engine, this particular 1853 version constructed with a single cylinder. Steam was generated in two boilers. On deck, Vaughan & Lynn set a pair of masts and rigged the steamship as a barque.[146]

Since the Philadelphia–Savannah line had ordered the *Keystone State* as a passenger transport, the ship contained forty-six staterooms, salons, a dining room, a ladies' parlor, a smoking room and a library, as well as running water in the washrooms.[147]

In the antebellum years after its launch in June 1853, there were several newspaper reports regarding the steamboat. In one night, while inbound to Philadelphia, the *Keystone* was hit by a small schooner at 10:00 p.m. and again a few hours later by another small craft. Both schooners sank; all but two of the crew members were rescued.[148] On a foggy night near Norfolk, the *Keystone State* hit the barque *Cavalier*. The steamer's bow was crushed, and it started taking on water. The captain was able to run the ship onto mudflats

A very busy waterfront, illustrated in *Bird's Eye View of Philadelphia 1850. Free Library of Philadelphia.*

in the harbor to keep it from sinking.[149] Another nighttime collision occurred in the Delaware River when the *Keystone* crashed into the barge *A. Groves, Jr.*, which was under tow behind a tug. The barge sank, and the owner sued the Philadelphia & Savannah Line. The case went all the way to the Supreme Court and reaffirmed maritime rules of right of way.[150]

Two more articles described engine failures due to broken side levers; in one instance, the *Keystone* became disabled seventy-five miles south of Cape Henlopen, which is the northern tip of the Delaware coast. It was towed to Norfolk, where passengers disembarked, and then towed back to Philadelphia for repair.[151]

The *Quaker City* became famous as the steamer that Mark Twain chartered for his "Innocents Abroad" voyage to the Holy Land, Egypt and Europe.

For the Cope Line, Vaughan & Lynn constructed *Tuscarora II*, *Tonawanda*, *Westmoreland* and *Lancaster*. When launching the *Tuscarora II* in February 1848, the Copes employed the *City Ice Boat* to clear the river, reimbursing the trustees twenty dollars. Other local firms that contributed to the ship's construction and received payment from H&A Cope were Reaney & Neafie for cutting blocks, I.P. Morris for a nozzle and George Landell for lumber.[152] As previously mentioned, Landell had been a Point Pleasant shipwright himself before converting his business to a lumberyard.

Charles Cramp assisted in producing seven passenger steamers in the 1850s for the Spanish Cuban government, the *General Armero*, *Carolina* and

Polynesian among them. They were intended for the West Indies trade. The *New York Times* published a story in April 1852 about a mishap that befell the *General Armero*, which had just been launched weeks before. The steamer was on its way to Havana when the starboard boiler "gave out" seventy miles south of Savannah. The ship was likely a side-wheeler, each wheel being driven by an engine and sometimes using multiple furnaces and boilers below deck. The short report does not detail how the *General Armero* was able to limp the distance to Charleston for repair without power to one side.[153] Perhaps another boiler was reconfigured to power engines on both sides or it made use of sails, which many steamers of that era carried.

Charles's father turned out six clippers in the same period. The fast-sailing clipper ships were involved in trade throughout the Pacific and California. In these peak years, it was estimated that William Cramp had about one hundred workers on his payroll.[154]

Francis Grice, chief naval architect for the U.S. Navy, was at this time reassigned to Philadelphia. After some of his ship designs were used in the War of 1812, he was appointed the naval constructor and moved to Gosport (Portsmouth), Virginia. Grice had short stints at the New York and Florida Navy Yards, returning to Pennsylvania in 1849. As the Civil War loomed,

Vaughan & Lynn launched *Tuscarora II* in 1848, destined for the Cope Line. *Daniel M. Dailey Collection.*

Tonawanda, built by Vaughan & Lynn for the Cope Line in 1850. *Free Library of Philadelphia.*

the loyalties of the longtime navy man likely came under suspicion due to his many southern relatives. His career ended in 1859 with his resignation.

His relative Francis, residing at 71 Queen Street, was employed as a machinist in 1846. The following year, a new business, S.B. & F. Grice & Company, began building steam engines at Beach Street between Hanover and Palmer, very near the location of Samuel Grice's lumber company.[155] Two younger members of the Grice family, Samuel B. and Francis, were probably the founders.

Increasing industrialization attracted many Europeans to Philadelphia. There were other forces pushing migrants across the Atlantic. The Great Famine of 1846 caused 750,000 desperate Irish to sail to American seaboard cities between the years 1845 and 1851.[156] At the Port of Philadelphia, there were 1,890 debarkations in 1835; five years later, the number was 4,079, and it rose to 19,211 in 1853.[157]

The city's environs grew at unprecedented rates. The center of the area's population was no longer located in the city, but rather it was north of Vine

Street. In the decade 1844–54, the number of people living in Philadelphia grew by 29.5 percent, while Spring Garden increased by 111.5 percent and Kensington's number jumped 109.5 percent.[158]

One steamship line and four lines of sailing packets linked Liverpool to Philadelphia, and in the summer, three ships per month transported people between Derry and the Delaware River.[159]

Tensions surrounding the immigrants' religious beliefs and competition for unskilled jobs surfaced in successive riots between 1834 and 1849. Warner states that these societal pressures show the interaction of important elements of the big-city era: industrialization, immigration, mixed patterns of settlement and the weakness of municipal institutions.[160] The movement for the consolidation of Kensington into the city of Philadelphia was partially a response to the lawlessness of the Nativist Riots.

In a larger sense, mid-nineteenth-century immigration was one of the most powerful factors in reshaping the city itself and the society residing within it.

William Sutton's offspring—Daniel, Edward, George and John—were shipwrights. The career of one member of the family, James T. Sutton (as with Samuel B. and Francis Grice), demonstrates the new opportunities open to the younger generations of shipwright clans. James T. operated a steam engine manufacturing company in 1841 on Franklin Street between Second and Front Street. At the same location, he built his own iron foundry to cast boilers for his engines; it was called Sutton & Smith. In 1845, the young industrialist merged the two firms to form the Franklin Iron Works.

Franklin Iron Works provided the engines for Sutton's uncle John Birely and cousin Theodore after the construction of the SS *Samuel S. Lewis*. The description from *Gleason's* magazine gave further details:

> *The new steamship was soon after hauled into the pier of the Franklin Iron Works of Messrs. James T. Sutton & Company, where her engines are in progress. The heaviest portion of her machinery is already on board, and her boilers are nearly ready to be shipped. The engines have cylinders of 60 inches diameter, with 40 inches stroke, working with 45 pounds of steam as high as 500 horsepower each. She will be completely fitted out here under the superintendence of Capt. Loper, one of her owners who is to deliver her in Boston about the latter end of July.*[161]

Loper and Birely coordinated with Franklin Iron Works again for the engines onboard the *Star of the South*. James T. Sutton and his business survived into the post–Civil War years.

Founded by James T. Sutton in 1845, Franklin Iron Works provided engines for Sutton's uncle John Birely. *World Digital Library*.

Birely's Ship Yard & Marine Railway business card. *Daniel M. Dailey Collection*.

As Vaughan & Lynn were experiencing their most productive years at the Shackamaxon Street wharf, Harmon Stout Vaughan and William Fisher established a yard nearby in 1851. The firm constructed the screw steamer *Peytona* and light vessels for the U.S. government during the Civil War.[162]

Reaney, Neafie & Levy began to experiment with iron shipbuilding. As propeller manufacturers, it preferred a metal hull that would withstand the vibrations the propeller's revolutions generated; vibration was a problem because it loosened engine bolts. In 1855, the company launched its first iron ship. Birely and Cramp assisted by supplying hull designs and supervising workers. Reaney departed at this point, but the two remaining partners, Jacob Neafie and John Levy, went on to construct three hundred more iron vessels in the next half century.[163]

As John K. Hammitt's son, John H., joined his father in a partnership, the elder Hammitt launched his namesake ship, the *John K. Hammitt*, as well as the *Rowena*.[164] They would be the last of his shipbuilding career. The Vaughan & Lynn partnership ended that year as well. These shipbuilders were victims of the Panic of 1857.

Chapter 14

THE ECONOMIC PANIC OF 1857 AND CIVIL WAR

The financial crash mid-century was worldwide. The Bank of Pennsylvania failed in September; it had a relationship with the state similar to that which the Bank of United States had previously held with the federal government. Suspension of specie payment occurred throughout the country but did not last into the next year. There was no extended depression, yet it was devastating to many businesses in Philadelphia, especially maritime affairs.

Tonnage of American cargo sold in foreign countries fell from sixty-five thousand tons in 1855 to seventeen thousand tons by 1860. Shipping between U.S. ports slowed in this same period; California became less dependent on imports from the East Coast. Shipbuilding came to a standstill.[165]

After the Panic, John K. Hammitt was reduced to working as a ship joiner and then briefly as a shipbuilder again, retiring in 1861. John H. leased the neighboring Kensington Screw Dock in 1860 for four years. At the Screw Dock, ships could offload on-site and then be lifted from the water for repairs. When it was sold, John H. continued working as a ship carpenter. The John K. Hammitt & Son shipyard declared bankruptcy in 1866. John H. died in 1872.[166]

Hammitt resided as a gentleman at 1014 Penn Street, which became North Delaware Avenue after the Consolidation of Philadelphia and subsequent renumbering, until his death in 1880.

Jacob K. Vaughan accepted a government position as supervising constructor for the U.S. Lighthouse Board under the Treasury Department. He oversaw repair and maintenance of lighthouses, and he also applied his shipbuilding skills to supervising the erection of many lightships for the board. At the time of his death in 1886, he and his wife were residing at 1222 Providence Road in Chester, Pennsylvania.[167]

Matthew Van Dusen passed away in 1856. Jacob Tees continued working as a shipwright to the end of his life in 1875. Samuel B. Grice switched to the timber business after his short-lived partnership with Francis.

Jacob Birely kept his Beach and Hanover Street yard functioning through the downturn and partnered with John W. Lynn from 1859 to 1862. Birely & Lynn constructed the *Phineas Sprague* and contracted with Merrick & Towne to provide engines.[168]

David Streaker was a Kensington shipwright who had formed a business with Charles Hillman; they built a cargo ship in 1853, as well as gunboats and light vessels for the navy.[169]

William Cramp's operations were also affected by the economic turbulence. He was forced to sell some of his assets to satisfy creditors. Sons Charles and William M. took control of the company, while their father gave his occupation as ship carpenter and acted as a foreman. In 1860, all three men returned to separate proprietorships.[170]

The Philadelphia & Reading Railroad piers at Port Richmond had expanded to eighteen by the time the Civil War began. From Barnes's map of 1861. *Historical Society of Frankford.*

In the decade before the crash, the Philadelphia & Reading Railroad bought twenty-two more riverfront acres. The Port Richmond piers now numbered eighteen and were capable of loading ninety vessels at one time. When P&R president Tucker began complaining about the lack of ships at Port Richmond, the company explored chartering and leasing vessels, finally deciding to purchase its own fleet. The first acquisition was the screw propeller steamer *Philadelphia*, constructed by Neafie & Levy.[171]

The South's threats of secession depressed Philadelphia's shipbuilding industry and its trade with the southern states, one of its most important markets. Neafie & Levy slowed construction of two iron ships for southern ports as concern about their potential use grew. When the Civil War began with the Confederate attack on Fort Sumter, the U.S. Navy swiftly ordered the Philadelphia Navy Yard to commence work on two new screw sloops and contracted with private yards and engine shops for gun boats. The navy, long reluctant to adapt its vessels to iron plating for protection and slow to see the advantage of screw propulsion over that of sidewheels, abruptly had to change policies at the outset of the war.[172] Kensington shipyards suddenly had so much work that they were competing with one another, and the Navy Yard, for workmen.

Throughout the four years of the Civil War, 152 merchant steamships were built. The U.S. Navy and U.S. Army also needed supply vessels and troop transports, and the Delaware River shipyards complied.

Early in the Civil War, John W. Lynn's business relocated to a wharf at Reed Street in South Philadelphia. Lynn, as well as Neafie & Levy, received contracts from a Philadelphia-Boston line that had sold its own steamships to the War Department.[173] Again, the Lynn family are significant for having had operations in both shipyard centers of the city.

Merrick & Sons submitted a proposal for an ironclad, which the navy accepted. John Towne had left the company to join I.P. Morris in the growing industrial district of Port Richmond. Samuel Merrick expanded with a wharf on the Delaware River and renamed the company Merrick & Sons, Southwark.[174] Merrick subcontracted with Cramp to construct the hull of the steam frigate USS *New Ironsides*, and Merrick's foundry was to provide its engines, boilers and masts. The vessel's iron plates were forged at Bailey, Brown & Company in Pittsburgh.[175] The famed USS *New Ironsides* was completed in August 1862 and launched to great fanfare.

Thanks to the success of this collaboration, Charles Cramp, his brothers and his father, William, recovered from debts their company had incurred after the Panic. The *New Ironsides* improved Cramp's reputation, and the

On stone by W. H Rease, 17, S.º 5th S.t Ph.ª

MERRICK & HIJO,
SUCCESSORES DE
MERRICK & TOWNE,
FILADELFIA.

Ingenieros y Fabricantes de Maquinas de Vapor, de Calderas, trapiches y de Maquinaria en general.

Ellos son tambien agentes exclusivos para la fabrica y la venta del martillo patente de vapor de accion directa de Nasmyth,—y del aparato ò maquina patente de Rillieux para cocer azucar.

ME
M

Engineers and Manufac
Machinery in general.

They are the exclusive
Patent Direct-action Stean
the Manufacture of Sugar

Merrick & Towne, established in 1835, built marine steam engines for Kensington ships.
Print & Picture Collection Free Library of Philadelphia.

Printed by *F. Kuhl, Ph.*

SON,

WNE,

nes and Boilers, Sugar Mills, and

ufacture and sale of Nasmyth's
Rillieux's Patent Apparatus for

MERRICK & FILS,

SUCCESSEUR DE

MERRICK & TOWNE,

PHILADELPHIE.

Ingénieurs et Fabricants de Machines à Vapeur, de Chaudières, moulin à cane
et de Machines et Appareilles en général.

Ils sont les agents exclusifs pour la fabrique et la vente du marteau à vapeur
à action directe (breveté) de Nasmyth,—et pour l' appareil (breveté) de Rillieux
pour la fabrication de sucre.

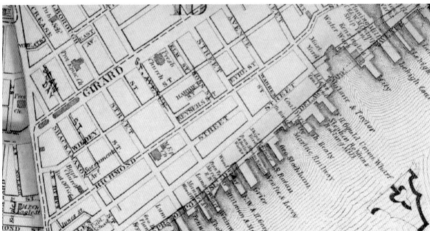

Top: Merrick & Sons subcontracted with Cramp to construct the USS *New Ironsides* in 1862 for the navy. *Daniel M. Dailey Collection.*

Bottom: On Barnes's map of 1865, piers of the Lehigh Coal & Navigation Company, the yard of Theodore Birely (who died the year prior) at Warren Street and Neafie & Levy, between Palmer and Hanover, are visible. *Free Library of Philadelphia.*

navy forwarded more contracts to the firm: a side-wheeler, another ironclad and the super cruiser USS *Chattanooga*. In 1864, Charles, William M. and William Sr. resumed joint management of the company, now formally named William Cramp & Sons, Shipbuilders.

The front of a *City of Richmond* advertisement. *Daniel M. Dailey Collection.*

William Sutton, after fifteen years in retirement, died in 1863. In 1864, Samuel B. Grice returned to steam engineering with a car manufacturing firm as horse-drawn street cars evolved into motor-driven passenger cars.

Joining two of the three surviving Kensington wooden shipbuilding yards, Birely, Hillman & Streaker was founded in 1865. Its consolidation could have been related to the death of Theodore Birely, at forty-six years of age in 1864, and the availability of the Birely shipyard on Warren Street. The address for Birely, Hillman & Streaker was 1441 Beach Street, which is the corner of Warren. The firm continued building steamships, using engines built by Neafie & Levy.

John Birely's life ended in August 1867. His obituary in the *Philadelphia Bulletin* described a gathering of gentlemen having a discussion at his home the night before he died. The only longtime business associate named in the article was Jacob Neafie.[176] His son, Jacob Birely, surely would have been among the company. These Kensington comrades, few of whom remained in the shipbuilding trades, might have reminisced about John's career spanning five decades and his influence on many of them. In December of the same year, Captain John Levy also died. Levy's heir, Edmund, took his place with partner Jacob Neafie.

During the war, a final mortal blow was dealt to the American clipper ship industry by Confederate cruisers. Their British-built, speedy wooden

NEW YORK
AND
LONG BRANCH!

THE ENTIRELY NEW AND FAST STEAMER
CITY OF RICHMOND,
CAPTAIN E. KEMBLE.

Built by BIRELY, HILLMAN & STREAKER, Philadelphia. Launched in June and completed in September, 1880.

THREE DAILY TRIPS! TWO TRIPS SUNDAYS!

TIME TABLE.
Commencing June 11th, 1881.
Leave NEW YORK:

Pier 3, N.R.: 5,00 A.M.; 11.00 A.M.; 3.45 P.M.

Sundays { Foot West 20th St.: 8.30 A.M.; 1.30 P.M.
{ Pier 3, North River: 9.00 A.M.; 2.00 P.M.

☞ BROOKLYN ANNEX BOAT, leaving Fulton Ferry 10.30 A.M., daily, and Sundays 8.30 A.M., connects with Steamer "City of Richmond."

Leave LONG BRANCH:

Ocean Pier: 7.45 A.M.; 1.15 P.M.; 6.15 P.M.
SUNDAYS: 11.30 A.M.; 5.00 P.M.

The N. Y. Transfer Company will call for and deliver Baggage.

The appointments of the Boat are first class in every particular. Attention is called to the Restaurant on the Main Deck, where everything is served in a style unsurpassed.

FARE, either way,.........................50 Cents.
Excursion Tickets, (good only on day sold,). 60 Cents.
Commutation, 1 month, $15.00.

The reverse side of the same advertisement. The *City of Richmond*, a paddlewheel steamboat, was built by Birely, Hillman & Streaker in 1880. *Daniel M. Dailey Collection.*

Penn Steam Engine & Boiler Works, commonly known as Neafie & Levy. Thomas Reaney left the business in 1859. *World Digital Library*.

steamers would chase every merchantman they discovered on the seas, burning those found to be from Northern ports. When freight insurance rates increased in response, Union shippers either couldn't afford to keep doing business or panicked, selling their vessels abroad. By 1865, 1,600 Union ships had been transferred to new ownership in Europe.[177]

Postwar, there existed such a glut of ships built or acquired by the U.S. Navy that orders for new construction declined drastically. When John W. Lynn completed the work that kept his yard fully functioning throughout the war years, there were no more contracts to be had. In February 1870, Lynn closed his Southwark shipyard,[178] and the venerable line of Lynn shipwrights ceased. In contrast with the difficulties of the local shipyards, the Philadelphia & Reading Railroad acquired its own colliers. By controlling its own transport, the railroad took another step toward making the P&R the largest cartel of the coastal coal trade. This was one area of commerce in which Philadelphia not only surpassed New York but also dominated nationally.

Pressure from railroad men forced a change in the state law to allow for joint ownership of railroads and mines. The company acquired 100,000 acres of upstate coal lands and began to control twenty-seven mines.[179] At the eastern terminus of its line, the P&R again contracted with Neafie & Levy build another screw steamer, the *Pusey*. Railroad managers also ordered steamers from Reaney & Son in Chester, Pennsylvania. Thomas Reaney had separated from his partners Neafie and Levy at the beginning of the Civil War and opened a yard with his son, William.

The P&R requested the Cramp shipyard construct six iron screw steam colliers. They were designed to have the capacity for one hundred tons of coal each. By 1874, the railroad owned a fleet of 14 colliers and 120 schooners and barges.

The Port Richmond Terminal had also grown by the postwar years; now there were twenty-one piers at which 175 ships could be loaded simultaneously. The terminal was so large that one thousand rail cars could be accommodated within the transshipment port. The P&R was shipping an astounding 2 million tons of coal annually.

As prosperous as the railroad company was at this point, it was about to embark on a period of aggressive corporate leadership under Franklin Gowen, the president of the P&R Railroad in 1871.[180]

The Pennsylvania Railroad had also extended its line to the Delaware River in South Philadelphia at Washington Avenue. Compounding the situation for steamships that were transporting cargo other than coal, the railroads were now carrying much of the nation's freight.

Chapter 15

NEAFIE & LEVY; BIRELY, HILLMAN & STREAKER; AND CRAMP

THE LAST OF THE KENSINGTON SHIPWRIGHTS

In 1870, as the economy began to recover, maritime trade increased, and coastal steamship companies were encouraged to improve their fleets. Philadelphia's Clyde Line awarded most of its contracts to Cramp. There were still problems with iron hulls: they were more expensive to build, they rusted, rivets cracked and hulls were less elastic. Only a few steamship operators had confidence enough to invest in their construction. William Clyde was one of those men. William and his father, Thomas, were both from Philadelphia. Thomas had founded the Clyde Steamship Company in the 1840s, became acquainted with Jacob Neafie and was an early proponent of John Eriksson's screw propulsion.

Cramp contracted with Neafie & Levy to build engines for the *Clyde* in 1870, but two years later, when Charles Cramp received an order and started designing the *George W. Clyde*, he drew plans for a compound engine and used his own yard to assemble it. This type of engine, invented in Glasgow in 1854, employed two cylinders, one of high-pressure directly from the boiler and the other powered by spent steam from the first cylinder. Recycling steam reduced coal consumption, making vessels more economical. This was the first installation of a compound engine in an American steamship.[181]

William Inman and his partners operated the Liverpool and Philadelphia Steamship Company. The Richardson brothers were Irish Quakers, involved with the family linen export business. In 1845, the Richardsons decided to start manufacturing linen in County Armagh near Belfast; their factory had one of the first steam-driven looms in Ireland. John Richardson hired a young partner, William Inman, to oversee the shipping section of the business.[182]

The family started their linen production just as the famine began. Irish farmers who had suffered crop loss needed work; the Richardsons saw the devastation the famine was causing and provided jobs. Inman convinced John and his brothers in 1850 to establish a steamship line, to run from Liverpool to Philadelphia. They purchased a new ship, iron hulled and screw propelled, from a yard in Glasgow. The partners were the first to transport poor immigrants in steerage by steamship. Inman and the Richardsons were concerned about the terrible conditions under which the Irish had been sailing to America. The line provided improved quarters and cooked meals for their passengers. After a successful first few years, William bought out his partners, and the Liverpool-Philadelphia Steamship Company became known as the Inman Line. Another innovation Inman instituted was to incorporate an outbound stop in Queenstown, County Cork, to save the impoverished travelers the added expense of having to cross the Irish Sea. This made the line so incredibly popular that Cunard built a departure from Ireland into its schedule three years later.[183]

The Pennsylvania Railroad's westbound passenger service had enjoyed the business the British Inman Line provided. After the immigrant transport line relocated its North American terminal from Philadelphia to New York in 1857, the Pennsylvania began to search for a new transatlantic steamship connection for the Philadelphia terminal. The railroad made unsuccessful attempts during the Civil War. In 1871, the Pennsylvania and a group of local investors proposed to back two new lines, the U.S.-flagged American Steamship Company and the foreign-flagged International Navigation Company. The plan was to coordinate sailings of the two lines on the Liverpool-Philadelphia route. The ASC's new corporate board sought bids from shipbuilders for four three-thousand-ton iron steamships. Four Delaware Valley yards submitted proposals: Neafie & Levy, John Roach in Chester, Dialogue & Wood in Camden and Cramp & Sons. The latter won the contract.

No American shipyard up to this point had constructed a vessel larger than 2,067 tons, a record established by Harlan & Hollingsworth in Wilmington, Delaware. None had yards that could accommodate the tonnage that British builders were achieving. In accepting the ASC contracts, Charles Cramp realized that this huge undertaking would require a major reorganization and new facilities. At the same time, Cramp's Palmer Street yards were busy constructing a steamship for the Clyde Line, as well as other overhauls. Charles looked north along the Delaware and found a large lot at the foot of

Norris Street, just south of the Port Richmond Terminal, that he could use as a second shipyard. Next, he applied to the state for permission to create a corporation. The proprietorship had now evolved into the incorporated William Cramp & Sons Ship & Engine Building Company. The new Norris Street yard contracted with ship iron suppliers in Reading and Pottstown and secured iron plates from the Pottsville Iron Works. Boilers and engines were to be built by Cramp specialists on site.

The American Steamship Company liners were named the Pennsylvania Class after the first such ship was completed. Compound engines drove a single propeller screw. ASC christened its four new ships the *Pennsylvania*, the *Ohio*, the *Illinois* and the *Indiana*, in honor of the states the Pennsylvania Railroad crossed. These vessels were launched as passenger liners in August and November 1872 and in March and June 1873.[184]

The American Line built wharves at Washington Avenue in Southwark. This was the same site the Navy Yard had occupied since 1800 but just vacated, and prior to that, it had been Joshua Humphreys's shipyard.[185] To ease the transfer of newly arrived travelers from the steamships, its terminal was located next to the Emigrant Station and the PRR tracks.

Iron shipbuilding had declined to its lowest point in the late 1870s. A general economic depression, triggered by the Panic in 1873, had dragged on for several years. In the year 1877, Neafie & Levy had no ship launchings; Cramp & Sons built one small tug on its own account. William Cramp, the founder of the organization, passed away in 1879. Charles was elected president of the company by his brothers.

Meanwhile, coastal steamship lines increasingly suffered from railroad competition. A Clyde subsidiary, the Philadelphia & New York Steam Navigation Company, discontinued service. The Philadelphia & Southern Mail Steamship Company, which had moved freight and passengers between ports along the Atlantic to New Orleans, closed its operations.

As domestic contracts diminished, Charles Cramp put his efforts into convincing the Department of the Navy to give Delaware Valley yards its repair business. The government did provide some contracts, but the navy was downsizing too. It had closed the old Washington Avenue yard, laid off its workers and not yet created its League Island facility.

Cramp was sustained by the large dry dock that had been installed at the old Palmer Street yard in 1875. The company had an overhaul division there to perform dry dock repairs, separate from its shipbuilding department. The largest steamers on the Delaware River could be towed into place, and then a floating caisson would close the dock and four huge

Right: Charles Cramp (1828–1913). *Daniel M. Dailey Collection*.

Below: *Pennsylvania*, one of four three-thousand-ton vessels that Cramp built for the American Steamship Company in 1872. *Daniel M. Dailey Collection*.

Ticket to view the launching of the *Chalmette* in 1879 at the Cramp shipyards. *Daniel M. Dailey Collection.*

steam pumps would remove the water at 120,000 gallons per minute. The Philadelphia & Reading Railroad colliers underwent annual inspections at the Cramp dry dock.[186]

Another source of work came from the Imperial Russian Navy, as it prepared for possible war with Britain. Cramp converted three American steamships for the Russian fleet, two were the *Columbus*, which became the *Europe*, and the *Saratoga*, which was reconfigured into the *Asia*. Both were small warships or corvettes of about three hundred feet.

The company also constructed another steamer for the Russian navy in 1880, the *Zabiaca*. It was known to be the fastest cruiser in the world. Each of these ships had compound engines and screw propellers.[187] These contracts were the start of a close relationship between Charles Cramp and the Imperial Russian Navy.

The situation had improved by 1883. Cramp secured contracts for the Hawaiian sugar trade and constructed three cotton steamers. Neafie & Levy built iron tugs and provided engines for Birely, Hillman & Streaker's wooden hulls.

Although William Clyde moved his company offices to New York in 1873, he continued to order iron steamers from Cramp and wooden steamers from Birely, Hillman & Streaker. The Clyde Line operated ten passenger and cargo lines between twenty-one East Coast cities.[188]

The most volatile force in the post–Civil War economy continued to be the railroads. Between 1870 and 1890, American railroad mileage tripled. Ever more expansive plans had been discussed within the Philadelphia & Reading Railroad since 1860. The company's London investors had suggested forming a Philadelphia–New York, a Philadelphia–West Indies and a transoceanic coal steamship line, none of which ever materialized. Another idea was that the P&R should have its own shipyard. A shipbuilding facility was built at Port Richmond in 1874 but was little utilized.

Through his stormy tenure as P&R president in the 1870s, Frank Gowen sought to undercut independent coal operators, convinced other

Opposite, top: Cramp converted three American steamships for the Imperial Russian Navy. The *Columbus* became the *Europe*. *Daniel M. Dailey Collection*.

Opposite, bottom: Cramp steamship *Columbus*. *Daniel M. Dailey Collection*.

Above: The Russian navy ordered another steamer from Cramp in 1880, the *Zabiaca*. *Daniel M. Dailey Collection*.

Colliers at Port Richmond in 1875. Coal trains can be seen on the docks in the distance. *Wikimedia Commons.*

coal executives to agree to price-fixing, manipulated transportation prices, reduced miners' wages to keep costs low and fought early union efforts when workers went on strike. He battled with investors and his own board of managers. The P&R was overextended and overinvested. It began a decline that resulted in bankruptcy in 1880.[189] Because of its level of debt, the company could not recover after the Panic of 1873. There were other factors Gowen refused to see—coal prices overall were falling, plus the center of ironmaking, and soon steelmaking, was moving to Pittsburgh, drawn by expanding markets in the Midwest.

Gowen remained the president and was even one of the receivers through the reorganization. A new group of investors, led by Anthony Drexel and J.P. Morgan, finally replaced Gowen. Morgan reorganized the P&R, and from that point on, Drexel, Morgan & Company became the chief financiers of the railroad.

In 1890, Archibald McLeod became president of the P&R Railroad. Even more reckless than Gowen had been, McLeod intended to dominate the anthracite mining and coal transportation industries and transform the Philadelphia & Reading into one of the country's premier lines. His focus was on expanding the rail network.

By early 1892, the railroad controlled 72 percent of anthracite production facilities in the country. J.P. Morgan forced local lines acquired by McLeod to reorganize under the Reading.

McLeod shocked railroad men by invading the territory of the New York Central and New England rail lines. This went against Morgan's philosophy that great railroads should protect their investors by cooperating with one another. In February 1993, McLeod's empire collapsed. The earnings of the

In "The Perspective of Philadelphia," Burk & McFetridge depict the Kensington waterfront from Neafie & Levy's yard to the Port Richmond coal depot in 1886. *Free Library of Philadelphia.*

overburdened P&R couldn't support the inflated payments due to owners of the many leased railroads. Rumors of its failure caused the company's stock to fall. Bankruptcy was declared. Drexel, Morgan & Company threatened to cut funding unless McLeod resigned. He did.

The U.S. Treasury's reserve had been shrinking, and confidence in the nation's economic health was already low; the failure of the Philadelphia & Reading pushed the country into another financial crisis. The railroad had grown so large that its collapse effected not only its own stock price but also hundreds of millions of dollars' worth of stocks and bonds of dependent trunk line systems, as well as coal companies—the engines of the U.S. economy.[190]

After J.P. Morgan rescued the company and it emerged from bankruptcy, the railroad was reduced to a regional carrier again. It lost its collier fleet but began to employ Philadelphian Lewis Luckenbach's Towboat Company tandem system, a single tug that towed a string of barges. After Luchenbach demonstrated that it could decrease shipping costs, he ordered more powerful vessels of greater than two hundred tons from Neafie & Levy. The P&R realized that this system could increase their tonnage and began to use it to transport coal coastally.[191]

In 1906, the passage of the Hepburn Act required railroads to disinvest themselves from mine operations.[192] The Reading had to sell the P&R Coal and Iron Company.

In the twentieth century, the Reading filed for bankruptcy one final time in 1971. Five years later, the Reading sold all its rail assets to Conrail, including the Port Richmond Terminal. The terminal was then dismantled.

Over its 130-year history, the P&R and then the Reading employed thousands of workers from the river wards at Port Richmond. There was stable work on the railroad and at the terminal in occupations such as train handlers, dock men, managers and engineers. From the beginning, Port Richmond attracted other businesses that found it beneficial to be located near the coal transshipping yard. I.P. Morris relocated south of the Richmond Terminal at York Street in the first decade of the port's existence, and Charles Cramp built his second shipyard near the terminal in 1871.

Chapter 16

THE NEW NAVY AND THE END
OF CRAMP FAMILY OWNERSHIP

Continuing losses caused the Pennsylvania Railroad to force the sale of the American Steamship Company to the International Navigation Company. Although the INC, headed by Clement Griscom, was set up as an American holding company, Griscom, with the approval of his financial backers, immediately sought and received an agreement from the Belgian government to base a steamship line in Antwerp. It was becoming apparent to some Americans, President Grant among them, that the country was losing the competition over oceangoing shipping. Sailing under a foreign flag was one strategy companies used to be able to operate within the European monopoly of the Atlantic.[193] The Antwerp–Philadelphia–New York line was called the Red Star; its fleet was British-built. Griscom also acquired the Inman Line not long after the PRR decided to get out of the steamship business.

At the same time, powerful forces began to advocate for rebuilding the navy. Appropriations were approved for four battleships in 1883 and more in 1886 and 1887. Cramp won five of the contracts: the protected cruisers USS *Baltimore*, the USS *Newark* and the USS *Philadelphia*; the gunboat USS *Yorktown*; and the "dynamite cruiser" USS *Vesuvius*.

After this work was completed, old customers gave Cramp new commissions. The Clyde Line ordered two passenger vessels. The Red "D" Line, the same firm for which John Hammitt built ships in the 1840s, needed new vessels for its Venezuelan trade. The Metropolitan Steamship Company, a New York–Boston line, and the Baltimore-based Merchants and Miners Transportation Company also contracted with Cramp for steamers.

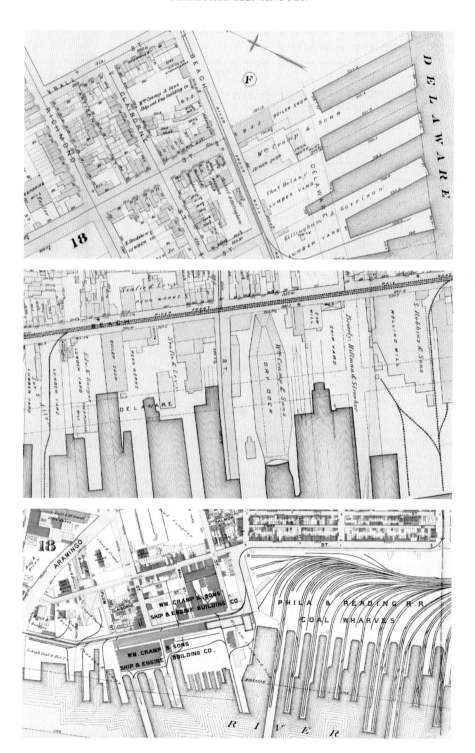

Opposite, top: Charles Cramp opened a second yard at the foot of Norris Street in 1872. Bromley 1887 Plate E. *Philadelphia Water Department.*

Opposite, middle: Birely, Hillman & Streaker was founded in 1865 on the Birely shipyard site at Warren Street. Cramp's large dry dock at the Palmer Street yard sustained the company during economic depressions. Bromley 1887 Plate C. *Philadelphia Water Department.*

Opposite, bottom: In Bromley's map of 1895, Plate 14, the size of the Cramp Shipyard and the Port Richmond Terminal, only half of which is shown, can be appreciated. *Athenaeum of Philadelphia.*

Above: Neafie & Levy stock certificate. *Daniel M. Dailey Collection.*

The Pacific Improvement Company's order of the *El Sol* was the first merchant vessel to exceed four thousand gross tons at four hundred feet in length. The *Iroquois*, built for William Clyde, was the first steel ship in the United States, demonstrating the shipyard's increasing use of steel in its hulls. The recent navy contracts had improved Cramp's capacity to the degree that the yard had few competitors for large vessel orders.

Demand for work improved for Neafie & Levy. Between 1888 and 1893, the firm constructed twenty-eight small iron steamships and thirty engines for wooden steamers. The company's most extraordinary creation was the *Corsair II* for J. Pierpont Morgan. The New York banker gave a friend, J. Fredrick Tams, carte blanche to spend on the elaborate steel yacht. At 240 feet, it was designed to have a sharp bow like a clipper, a black hull, private cabins, a library and elegantly furnished social rooms. Encouraged by the steady contracts, the cautious owners Jacob Neafie and Edmund Levy expanded their offices and workshops and made the decision to incorporate.

The economic climate convinced Charles Hillman to buy out his partners Jacob Birely and David Streaker to establish Hillman & Sons in 1888. Under the new management, the yard finally ceased constructing wooden hulls. Hillman began building tug engines and launched the *Anthony Groves*, an iron steamer.

Significantly, the five Cramp brothers—Charles, William, Samuel, Jacob and Theodore—who up to this point were not only the directors of the company but also held all its stock, began to sell shares to outside investors. Even though they still held 30 percent of the total, this was the final step in the Cramp family's loss of proprietorship.[194]

One of the new shareholders and board members was Clement Griscom, president of International Navigation Company. When Congress, under pressure from a maritime reform coalition, passed a bill that would grant subsidies to American ships for each mile sailed in the foreign trade, Griscom lobbied to be able to apply for funds. Initially deemed ineligible for the subsidy because his ships were built in England and registered in Belgium, special legislation eventually did authorize U.S. registry for the INC's two largest vessels in a deal in which Griscom agreed to give a significant commission to an American shipyard. Not surprisingly, contracts went to Charles Cramp for two transatlantic passenger liners in 1892.

The *St. Paul* and the *St. Louis* were constructed for the American Steamship Company, the still-operational subsidiary the INC had acquired from the Pennsylvania Railroad eight years earlier.

Meanwhile, the navy was preparing to upgrade its Civil War–era fleet. Cramp was awarded four contracts out of five for the USS *New York*, USS *Indiana*, USS *Massachusetts* and USS *Columbia*. The *New York Times* reported, "William Cramp & Sons have now on hand the greatest undertaking in the history of American shipbuilding. Four great warships, the largest vessels ever built in the United States, and designed to be the most powerful fighting ships in the world, must be launched, tried, and turned over to the government in three years' time." To prepare for the work, the firm purchased I.P. Morris, renamed Port Richmond Iron Foundry, its previous subcontractor. Such acquisitions to improve its facilities, however, increased company debt.

Aerial view of Cramp Shipyard. *From left to right*: cruiser *Minneapolis*, battleship M*assachusetts*, battleship *Iowa*, *St. Louis*, armed cruiser *Brooklyn*, *St. Paul* and battleship *Indiana*. *Daniel M. Dailey Collection*.

The *St. Paul*, constructed by Cramp for the American Steamship Company, then a subsidiary of the International Navigation Company. *Daniel M. Dailey Collection*.

Port Richmond Iron Foundry. *Free Library of Philadelphia.*

Built by Cramp & Sons, the USS *New York* took part in the blockade of Cuba ordered by President McKinley. This action precipitated the Spanish-American War. From *Our Country in War* by Murat Halstead. *Wikimedia Commons.*

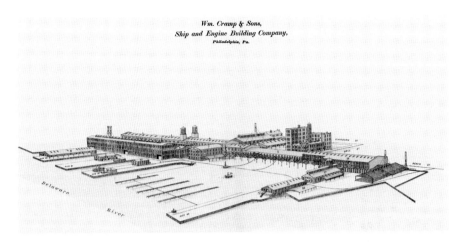

Wm. Cramp & Sons' shipyard piers between Norris and York Streets in 1893. *Free Library of Philadelphia.*

During the Civil War, a source of plating for the *New Ironsides* had been a Pittsburgh foundry. In the decades following the war, the relationship between eastern and western Pennsylvania grew exponentially thanks to the PRR. Production from Pittsburgh's blast furnaces and rolling mills was sent to Philadelphia's machine shops, locomotive factories and rail mills.

By 1890, Cramp was using Carnegie steel transported by the PRR. The need to upgrade from iron to steel, however, made the Kensington company susceptible to whatever affected the supply chain at the other end of the state such as labor strikes and material changes from steel plates to nickel-steel for armor. After Cramp riveters installed steel plates on the USS *New York*, the navy decided that it preferred composite nickel-steel. The steel deck plates had to be unscrewed and replaced. Compounded with delays caused by naval inspectors, the roiling societal and industrial events brought Cramp to the brink of failure.

Despite these serious issues, the company accepted contracts for four more cruisers and battleships: USS *Minneapolis*, USS *Alabama*, USS *Brooklyn* and USS *Iowa*. Charles Cramp had little choice. Due to the Panic of 1893, he did not expect his company to receive enough merchant marine orders to boost the Cramp finances. The Hillman & Sons shipyard had not fared well with its navy contract and declared bankruptcy.[195] And Jacob Birely, the last of an influential shipwright line that extended back almost one hundred years, died in 1895.

The new navy vessels would soon be called into service. U.S. shipping firms had long been active in commerce in South America and the Caribbean.

By the 1890s, they were interested in Central America for its trade and the possible access to the West Coast by canal. But the most lucrative ventures were in Cuba. After the Civil War, American businessmen controlled the sugar market on the island. Even though a Spanish governor general presided over the colony, the United States was the economic power.

The Cuban war for independence began in 1895. Rebels were attacking Spanish troops and burning sugar plantations. In early April 1898, President McKinley demanded that Spain grant an armistice to the insurrectionists, following that with another demand to evacuate Spanish forces. Without waiting long for a response, on April 22 the president ordered a blockade of the Cuban coast to protect American property on the island. Because of this direct threat, Spain declared war; the U.S. Congress responded in kind. The American navy's priority was to confront the Spanish squadron.

Battleships that the navy had contracted from Cramp were involved in the blockade of Santiago de Cuba: the USS *New York*, USS *Massachusetts* and USS *Columbia*. In the decisive sea battle, three of the five American ships that destroyed the Spanish vessels were built by Cramp: the USS *Indiana*, the USS *Iowa* and the USS *Brooklyn*.

Spain sued for peace in August and lost its colonies, the Philippines, Guam and Puerto Rico to the United States in the treaty negotiations. Cuba gained its independence, with many imposed restrictions, and the American-owned sugar cane plantations and refineries were back in business. The United States emerged from the short war as a major naval power.[196]

By October, the Cramp shipyards in Kensington had launched the first of three steamers in three years for the New York and Cuba Mail Steamship Company. After Spain lost Cuba, the line experienced an increased demand for passenger and freight service to the island.

Seven years later, in 1900, American steel shipbuilding had its most productive year and finally surpassed wooden construction. Much work came to Cramp: the Imperial Russian Navy requested a battleship and a protected cruiser, the United Fruit Company purchased four steamers, the New York & Cuba Mail Steamship Company ordered nine vessels, the Clyde Line awarded the firm another nine contracts and Cramp craftsmen built the ornate *Kroonland* and *Finland* for the International Navigation Company. These two passenger liners had first-class accommodations that boasted dining halls for 250 people, drawing rooms with green silk tapestry and satinwood tables and smoking rooms paneled with oak.[197]

Charles Cramp continued to cultivate his relationship with the Imperial Russian Navy since the work the yard had completed in 1880. It paid off

Cramp's *Atlas*, a floating derrick, built in 1892, is shown at Chestnut Street in this photograph from 1898. *PhillyHistory.org*

in 1898 when the Russian navy called on his company to assist in updating its vessels, and the *Retvizan* was ordered. Captain Schensnovich was sent to Philadelphia to oversee construction of the battleship and a cruiser, the *Variag*. During his stay in the city, Charles invited the captain and his officers to a dinner party that included Lloyd Bankson, the shipyard's naval constructor, at the Bellevue Hotel.[198] Charles Cramp again had to upgrade and expand the company's facilities. For that purpose, he purchased the defunct Hillman yard.

After Jacob Neafie died in 1898, the fortunes of Neafie & Levy declined. Neafie's will assigned his shipyard holdings to a trustee, who sold a large number of shares to a marine engineer. Even though neither had business experience, they aggressively booked many contracts and then found it difficult to complete orders due to their initial low bids.

Matthias Seddinger, the trustee, became the president of the company. He and Sommers Smith, the marine engineer, built tugs and other vessels for the Reading Railroad, the U.S. Navy, the City of Philadelphia and the Standard Oil Company. One of the Standard Oil tugs, completed in 1902 and given the name S.O. CO. NO. 14, is still operational and can be found on the Delaware waterfront near Independence Seaport Museum. It was renamed *Jupiter* in 1939 and is currently owned and maintained by the Philadelphia Ship Preservation Guild.

The blow to the company's reputation came when a year-old steamer, the *City of Trenton*, suffered a boiler explosion that killed twenty-four passengers in one of the worst steamboat disasters on the Delaware River. By 1904, Neafie & Levy was in receivership. It was sold four years later. The owners delivered one last tug, the *Adriatic*, and then discontinued shipbuilding. The machine shops and buildings at Beach and Palmer Streets were torn down and the berths dismantled. Nothing remained of the respected Neafie & Levy–Penn Works, where three hundred ships and one thousand marine engines were constructed in its seventy years of business.

In 1902, even the esteemed William Cramp & Sons Ship & Engine Building Company was on the verge of default. Charles sought loans, but at that same time, markets were contracting after the boom in 1900. During negotiations, the bankers asked for the resignations of the current directors. Charles resigned in October 1903.[199]

Augustus Buell, a William Cramp & Sons employee and biographer, worked with Charles during his forced retirement to write the history of the company under his management. Titled *The Memoirs of Charles H. Cramp*, it was published in 1906.

On June 17, 1913, both the *Philadelphia Inquirer* and the *New York Times* had front-page headlines announcing, "CHARLES H. CRAMP, WORLD FAMED AS SHIPBUILDER, DIES." The obituary described that Charles had expired at noon the previous day after a lingering illness. His death occurred at the residence of his son, William D. Cramp. He was eighty-five years old.

The *Philadelphia Inquirer* stated, "Perhaps no American has ever enjoyed a more widespread reputation in the business and industrial world than did Mr. Cramp. In every part of the civilized world, he was recognized as

Mr. Charles H. Cramp
requests the pleasure of
Naval Constructor, L. Bankson, U.S.N.
company at the Bellevue to dinner
on Saturday, March eighth at seven-thirty o'clock,
to meet
Captain Edward N. Stchensnovitch
and Officers of the Battleship "Retvizan,"
also Members of the Board of Inspection,
Imperial Russian Navy.

An early answer is requested to
507 South Broad Street.

Above: The Imperial Russian Navy contracted with Charles Cramp for the *Retvizan* and the *Variag*. Captain Schensnovich was sent to Philadelphia to oversee the work. Cramp hosted a dinner for the captain at the Bellevue Hotel, sending the Russians this engraved invitation. *Daniel M. Dailey Collection.*

Right: *Jupiter* tugboat, built by Neafie & Levy in 1902. Currently owned and operated by Philadelphia Ship Preservation Guild. *Photo by Gretchen Bell.*

one of the foremost naval architects of his day, while to him, more than to anyone else, was probably due the credit of developing shipbuilding in the United States."[200] In the Quaker-influenced city, not prone to hyperbole, this was high praise.

The firm continued under new management, taking navy and various passenger liner contracts. It revived with increased demand during World War I and then closed after launching its last ship in 1927, a victim of a postwar maritime depression. Cramp subsidiaries, one of which was the I.P. Morris Company, were sold to the Baldwin Locomotive Works. With the approach of the Second World War, the secretary of the navy reopened the site. After an extensive cleanup, reconditioning of the plant and hiring and training tens of thousands of workers, William Cramp & Sons reemerged to contribute to the war effort. When its last order of cruisers was completed, a year after peace was established, the company closed permanently.[201] The whole complex was demolished in the 1960s, with the exception of the Machine & Turret Shop on Richmond Street. The machine shop demolition would happen in the twenty-first century to make way for yet another I-95 expressway on-ramp.

EPILOGUE

On a perfect spring morning in May 1873, the day of the launch of the *Pennsylvania*, William Cramp spoke to a crowd of dignitaries aboard the new liner. He told the gathering that the new steamship was the crowning achievement of his career, which had begun on that same day fifty years prior, when he received his indenture as a journeyman ship carpenter.[202]

On that day, the man who could claim that his company was the only surviving American shipbuilding company to make the transition from sail and wood, to iron and steam, spoke with justifiable pride of his accomplishments. Success still lay ahead for his son Charles. But soon, for the Cramp family, and all the interconnected and interrelated shipwright families, the era of the Kensington maritime enterprise would be at an end. The arc of the rise and fall of Kensington shipbuilding spanned little more than 150 years. All the shipyards closed or evolved into other businesses.

By 1863, 45 percent of British emigrants to America had traveled by steam power. Three years later, the number rose to 80 percent.[203] The carriers were not Philadelphia-built ships; most were not American made. They were British and German.

The Cope Line struggled after the 1857 depression and the Civil War. Thomas P. Cope's sons, Henry and Alfred, had taken over the shipping business under the name H&A Cope. They, in turn, stepped aside for Henry's sons, Francis Reeve and Thomas P. Cope, who then controlled the packet line and renamed it Cope Brothers. The company never made the transition to steam and, as a result, lost business to those that did convert. Postwar,

William Cramp (1807–1879), founder of Wm. Cramp & Sons. *Daniel M. Dailey Collection.*

there was no doubt that New York was the preferred port. The Copes were also hurt by competitively low freight rates and the high cost of insurance. After providing passenger and freight service between Philadelphia and Liverpool for fifty years, the Cope brothers ceased the packet line in the mid-1870s and sold their ships.[204]

The New York Collins line in addition to Enoch Train's Boston shipyard were both driven out of business by the depression.

Belgium and France began to build steamships in 1853 and 1854. The German Hamburg-America Line, which survived longer than the Belgian and French companies and became very successful, switched from sail to steam in 1856.[205]

Most of the Atlantic steamship service in the late 1850s was provided by the Cunard Line and the Germans. The British had been moving quickly ahead. This was partially a credit to marine engineering and iron hull construction; however, there was also a government policy of subsidizing private steamship lines. Parliament believed that it was important for the nation to maintain the premier international shipping network.

By 1870, there were only six shipyards in America able to turn out iron ships.[206] Cramp and Neafie & Levy were among those few.

Philadelphia made up for the loss of mercantile trade and immigrant transport by becoming the primary transshipment port for Pennsylvania coal. The Reading Railroad's use of iron colliers for moving its product, and the preference for freighting agriculture and manufactured goods westward via the Pennsylvania Railroad, spelled the end of Kensington wooden shipbuilding.

Kensington shipyards, mostly begun on a small pre-industrial scale by individual shipwrights, either moved toward construction of larger ships of steam and steel or failed to adapt and shuttered. By the mid-nineteenth century, the full effect of the Industrial Revolution was engaged. Only Cramp, and for a short time Neafie & Levy, had the business acumen and technological capability to be able to progress to the next phase: manufacturing on a massive scale.

All the mechanical innovation—such as curved-blade propellers, screw propulsion and compound steam engines—created in these neighborhood yards were absorbed into the great Philadelphia factories of Baldwin and Stetson and, eventually, applied in shipyards the world over.

Then Philadelphia began to forget its historic maritime industry. Citizens lost the memory of who had constructed the city's merchant marine and where the great launchings, which were huge public events, had occurred. Vessels that ship lines had depended on to transport people and products across the Atlantic and along the eastern coast since their colonial beginnings were no longer the only means of moving freight. Other shipyards continued; across the river in Camden, New York Shipyard was successful, and downriver in Delaware County and Wilmington, Sun Ship and Harlan & Hollingsworth, respectively, had notable legacies. The only memory of the Kensington shipwrights was retained by family documentarians such as Charles Cramp, Captain Van Deusen and David Gauer, a Vaughan descendant. And the cemeteries.

NOTES ON SOURCES

1. Philadelphia City Directories were the key to pulling all the pieces of this story together. Confirmation of the existence of shipwrights, along with their mostly male relatives of the same last name, could be obtained from this primary source material. City directories were published annually. These small journals provided an individual's first and last name, cross streets or address of residence, the person's stated occupation and, for business owners, often the company address. Shipwright partnerships also could be found in the directories. If a man retired, his occupation changed to "gentleman." These details are not in the end notes because the source seemed obvious and adding these would have compounded the already large number of references.

Rich Remer and I built a database of five thousand entries by combing through each year from 1785 to 1867, searching for the major shipwright family names. Philadelphia City Directories can be found online at philageohistory.org.

2. I found *Philadelphia Customs District: Vessel Data Taken from Surveyor's Certificates, Shipbuilder's & Master Carpenter's Certificates, 1793–1799* at Mystic Seaport's G.W. Blunt White Library. Two to a page, each of these forms has "Shipbuilding Industry" and "Custom House Basement Room No. 10" printed on them. The Custom House moved to the current location in 1934. I think it is likely that the move had to occur quickly at the end of a working day in order that the office be open on the next business day. Rich Remer told me that Marion Brewington discovered that the Custom

House administrator ordered massive amounts of either these forms or the original certificates to be disposed of, and Brewington managed to save a small amount of vessel data.

Mr. Brewington and his wife lived in Philadelphia for a time in the 1930s and later relocated to Connecticut. The couple gifted this source, along with other items, to Mystic Seaport.

I also visited the National Archives seeking master carpenter certificates completed by Kensington shipwrights. The D.C. NARA holds all vessel documentation prior to 1900. In Washington, I only found *one* Kensington master carpenter certificate, and that was for the steamboat *Delaware*, built by Joseph and Francis Grice in 1813.

From https://www.archives.gov/research/maritime/vessel-documents. html comes an explanation of Custom House vessel documentation:

REQUIRED VESSEL DOCUMENTATION
Certificate of Registration—required if the owner was engaged in foreign trade
Certificate of Enrollment—required if the ship was greater than twenty tons and intended for coastal trade
License—required for smaller vessels of five to twenty tons and intended for coastal trade

Systems for registering and measuring vessels date back to the English Navigation Laws of Charles II in 1660. These laws required vessels to be measured and registered to determine their national character, provide a basis for taxation and protect against foreign shipping and shipbuilding.

Douglas L. Stein described master carpenter certificates in *American Maritime Documents 1776–1860*, published by the Mystic Seaport Museum in 1992:

> *A master carpenter certificate was procured from the customhouse once the construction of a new vessels was finished. It was completed and signed by the builder or carpenter. These tradesmen were to record the vessel's name, measurements, the place and year of construction, and the names of the original owners. The vessel could then, if necessary, be moved from where it was built to where it was to be registered or sold. This document was required before any registration or enrollment could be issued, since it established a ship's origin and ownership.*

NOTES

Introduction

1. Brewington, "Maritime Philadelphia," 93–94.

Chapter 1

2. Rich Remer recordings, March 20, 2014.
3. Kyriakodis, *Philadelphia's Lost Waterfront*, 14; Dunn and Dunn, "Founding, 1681–1701," 5.
4. Digging 195, "Historical Context"; Soderlund, *Lenape Country*, 6, 15–16.
5. Steiner, "Pennsylvania Fishes."
6. Remer, "Fishtown and the Shad Fisheries," 20.
7. *Philadelphia Region When Known as Coaquannock*, map, 1934, Historical Society of Pennsylvania Map Collection, call number of 610 1654.
8. Weslager, *New Sweden on the Delaware*, 24–25, 31, 58.
9. Craig, "Peter Gunnarsson Rambo," 1–2.
10. Weslager, *New Sweden on the Delaware*, 62, 68, 99, 105, 112–26.
11. Craig, "Chronology"; Digging 195, "Historical Context."
12. Soderlund, *Lenape Country*, 18, 118.
13. Bronner, "Indian Deed for Petty's Island," 111–14.
14. Milano, *History of Penn Treaty Park*, 17–19.
15. Craig, "Chronology."

Chapter 2

16. Maddocks, "Atlantic Crossing," 39.
17. Brewington, "Maritime Philadelphia," 103–4.

18. Cotter, Roberts and Parrington, *Buried Past*, 227–29.
19. Yamin, *Digging in the City of Brotherly Love*, 135.
20. Remer and Milano, "Kensington and the Founding of Philadelphia," 9.
21. Carousso, "Esther King of Philadelphia," 120–26.

Chapter 3

22. Remer and Milano, "Kensington and the Founding of Philadelphia," 9.
23. Carousso, "Esther King of Philadelphia," 269–71.
24. Brewington, *Shipcarvers of North America*.
25. Farley, *To Commit Ourselves to Our Own Ingenuity*, 11.
26. Remer, "Old Kensington," 8–9.
27. Hardy, "Fish or Foul," 511–12.
28. Remer, "Old Kensington," 9.
29. *Plan of Property in Kensington by Lewis Evans* (original 1750), photocopy, Historical Society of Pennsylvania Map Collection, call number of 621 (1750)P.
30. Gillingham, "Some Colonial Ships Built in Philadelphia," 170.
31. Gauer, *Vaughan Shipwrights of Kensington*, 17–21.
32. *Pennsylvania Gazette*, November 11, 1742.
33. Farley, *To Commit Ourselves to Our Own Ingenuity*, 25–27.
34. Remer files; Leach, "Old Eyre House."
35. Milano, *Palmer Cemetery*, 12.

Chapter 4

36. Farley, *To Commit Ourselves to Our Own Ingenuity*, 21–23.
37. Carousso, "Esther King of Philadelphia," for Jeremiah Elfreth, 157, 162; for Joseph Lynn, 269–71, 278–79.
38. Leach, genealogical data and correspondence relating to old Philadelphia families.
39. Crowther, "Shipbuilding Output of the Delaware Valley," 93.
40. Ibid.
41. Keyser, "Colonel Jehu Eyre," 418.
42. Leach, genealogical data and correspondence.
43. Leach, "Old Eyre House."
44. Jackson, *Pennsylvania Navy*, 308–9, 318.
45. Leach, genealogical data and correspondence.

Chapter 5

46. Miller, "Federal City," 157.
47. Bower, *Bower Family of Philadelphia*, 8–9.
48. Rich Remer, personal research files.
49. Autobiography of Joseph Grice, Historical Society of Pennsylvania.

50. Rosen, *Most Powerful Idea in the World*, 20, 23, 28–29, 42, 104, 111, 161, 170, 186.
51. Ferguson, *Oliver Evans*, 12–13.
52. Sutcliffe, *Steam*, 27, 28.
53. American Philosophical Society, www.amphilsoc.org.
54. Sutcliffe, *Steam*, 29, 42, 44–47.
55. Watson, *Annals of Philadelphia*, 2:451.
56. Sutcliffe, *Steam*, 48.
57. Watson, *Annals of Philadelphia*, 2:451.
58. Sutcliffe, *Steam*, 29, 42, 44–48, 67–69, 127.
59. Allen, *James Rumsey*, 28–29.

Chapter 6

60. Hopkinson, *Miscellaneous Essays and Occasional Writings*, vol. 2.
61. Gelber, *Dragon and the Foreign Devils*, 166.
62. Brewington, "Maritime Philadelphia," 109.
63. Hoyt, "Wreck of the 'Philosopher' Helvetius," 69.
64. Brewington, *Philadelphia Customs District*.
65. Remer, personal research files.
66. Goldstein, *Philadelphia and the China Trade*, 35, 41.
67. Leach, genealogical data and correspondence.
68. Brewington, *Philadelphia Customs District*.
69. Leach, genealogical data and correspondence.
70. Brewington, *Philadelphia Customs District*.
71. Gauer, *Vaughan Shipwrights of Kensington*, 9–10, 23, 27, 30.
72. Dorwart, *Invasion and Insurrection*, 189.
73. Miller, "Federal City," 200.
74. Remer, recordings, November 11, 2015.
75. Remer, personal research files.
76. Brewington, *Philadelphia Customs District*.
77. Ibid.

Chapter 7

78. Ferguson, *Oliver Evans*, 30, 33.
79. Iles, *Leading American Inventors*, 9, 12–13.
80. Sutcliffe, *Steam*, 101, 109–11, 115, 144, 169–74, 179–80.
81. Ferguson, *Oliver Evans*, 36–41, 45–47, 51, 63.

Chapter 8

82. Remer, personal research file.
83. Daughan, *If by Sea*, 321.

84. Richardson, "Athens of America," 234.
85. Weightman, *Industrial Revolutionaries*, 109–10.
86. Gauer, *Vaughan Shipwrights of Kensington*, 74.
87. Bower, *Bower Family of Philadelphia*, 20.
88. Robson, *Biographical Encyclopaedia of Pennsylvania*, 370–71.
89. *Poulson's American Daily Advertiser*, 1806 and 1811, newsbank.com; *New York Gazette*, 1808, newsbank.com.
90. Van Deusen, *Van Deursen Family*, 176–77.
91. City Archives, Philadelphia County, Deed Book D, 68, 268.
92. Gauer, *Vaughan Shipwrights of Kensington*, 9, 10, 27, 36.

Chapter 9

93. Daughan, *If by Sea*, 414.
94. Doerflinger, *Vigorous Spirit of Enterprise*, 342.
95. Brewington, "Maritime Philadelphia," 111.
96. Harrison, *Philadelphia Merchant*, 200–201.
97. Cope family papers, Historical Society of Pennsylvania, collection 1486.
98. Gauer, *Vaughan Shipwrights of Kensington*, 36.
99. Walther, *Happenings in Ye Olde Philadelphia*.
100. Chandler, *Early Shipbuilding in Pennsylvania*, 33–34.
101. Scharf and Westcott, *History of Philadelphia*, 2,262.
102. Henry, *Eminent and Representative Men*, 456.
103. Gauer, *Vaughan Shipwrights of Kensington*, 11, 73, 75, 186.
104. Brewington, "Maritime Philadelphia," 111.

Chapter 10

105. Farr and Bostick, *Shipbuilding at Cramp & Sons*, 53.
106. Ibid., 8.
107. Miller and Sharpless, *Kingdom of Coal*, 13, 15, 16, 20, 22, 23, 25, 29, 30.
108. Fisher, "Maritime History of the Reading," 162–67.
109. Geffen, "Industrial Development and Social Crisis," 322.
110. Warner, *Private City*, 104.
111. Jordan, *Colonial and Revolutionary Families*, 68.
112. Hurd, *History of New London County, Connecticut*, 646.
113. Duffield, *Neafie & Levy Ship and Engine*, 4–5.
114. Bower, *Bower Family of Philadelphia*; In Search of Nothing, "History 101"; Milano, "Samuel Bower's Shipyards at Point Pleasant, Kensington."

Chapter 11

115. Heinrich, *Ships for the Seven Seas*, 17.

116. Buell, *Memoirs of Charles H. Cramp*, 40–41.
117. Remer, personal research file.
118. Tanner, *Stranger's Guide*.
119. Wainwright, "Age of Nicholas Biddle," 270, 287.
120. Cope family papers.
121. Milano, *Supplement to the History of the Kensington Soup Society*, 25.
122. *Public Ledger*, October 11, 1848.
123. Van Deusen, *Van Deursen Family*, 301–2.
124. Jordan et al., *Encyclopedia of Pennsylvania Biography*, 15:150.
125. City of Philadelphia, Department of Records, City Archives, Record Group 153, Bureau of Trustees of Ice Boats, 153.2, Account Journal, and 153.3, Receipt Notices.
126. Independence Seaport Museum collections.
127. U.S. Department of the Treasury, "Steam-Engines," 148–67.

Chapter 12

128. Duffield, *Neafie & Levy Ship and Engine*, 4–5.
129. Thompson, "Iron & Steel Shipbuilding Data Set, 10–11.
130. Farr and Bostick, *Shipbuilding at Cramp & Sons*, 9, 53.
131. Milano, *Supplement to the History of the Kensington Soup Society*, 3.
132. *Philadelphia Bulletin*, August 23, 1867.
133. Remer, personal files.
134. Geffen, "Industrial Development and Social Crisis," 324.
135. Remer, personal files.
136. *Philadelphia Public Ledger*, July 11, 1851, 2.
137. Fisher, "Maritime History of the Reading," 168–69.

Chapter 13

138. Heinrich, *Ships for the Seven Seas*, 24.
139. Online Archive of California, "Guide to the Union Cargo Manifests."
140. Maritime Heritage Project, "Steamships, Ship Passengers and Sea Captains."
141. "Launch of Steamer S.S. Lewis," framed sketch, Independence Seaport Museum collections.
142. Jackson, *Maritime History and Survey*, 272.
143. *Weekly Journal of Commerce*, December 30, 1852.
144. Ridgely-Nevitt, *American Steamships on the Atlantic*.
145. Gauer, *Vaughan Shipwrights of Kensington*, 75.
146. *Charleston Courier*, September 20, 1853, 2.
147. *Philadelphia Inquirer*, September 20, 1853, 1.
148. *Trenton State Gazette*, May 14, 1855, 2.
149. *New York Herald*, May 27, 1856.

150. *United States Reports: Cases Adjudged in the Supreme Court*, 63 US 461 (1859) (1885) (Washington, D.C.: U.S. Government Printing Office).
151. *New York Herald*, September 7, 1857, 4.
152. Cope family papers.
153. *New York Times*, April 21, 1852.
154. Farr and Bostick, *Shipbuilding at Cramp & Sons*, 8.
155. Remer, personal files.
156. Clark, *Irish in Philadelphia*, 36.
157. Warner, *Private City*, 138.
158. Geffen, "Industrial Development and Social Crisis," 360.
159. Clark, *Irish in Philadelphia*, 32, 34.
160. Warner, *Private City*, 125.
161. "Launch of Steamer S.S. Lewis."
162. Gauer, *Vaughan Shipwrights of Kensington*, 75.
163. Heinrich, *Ships for the Seven Seas*, 20, 22.
164. Remer, personal files.

Chapter 14

165. Whipple, "Clipper Ships," 113.
166. Remer, personal files.
167. Helffenstein, *Pierre Fauconnier and His Descendants*, 77.
168. Heinrich, *Ships for the Seven Seas*, 19.
169. Colton, "Hillman Ship & Engine Building."
170. Farr and Bostick, *Shipbuilding at Cramp & Sons*, 8.
171. Fisher, "Maritime History of the Reading," 169, 172.
172. Laing, *Seafaring America*, 297.
173. Heinrich, *Ships for the Seven Seas*, 25–26.
174. Bishop, *History of American Manufactures*, 26.
175. Heinrich, *Ships for the Seven Seas*, 38.
176. *Philadelphia Bulletin*, August 23, 1867.
177. Whipple, "Clipper Ships," 112, 113.
178. Heinrich, *Ships for the Seven Seas*, 33.
179. Miller and Sharpless, *Kingdom of Coal*, 81.
180. Fisher, "Maritime History of the Reading," 173–74.

Chapter 15

181. Heinrich, *Ships for the Seven Seas*, 19, 53.
182. Dictionary of Ulster Biography, "John Grubb Richardson."
183. Tute, *Atlantic Conquest*, 64–65.
184. Heinrich, *Ships for the Seven Seas*, 55–57, 59, 61–64.
185. Kyriakodis, *Philadelphia's Lost Waterfront*, 123–25.

186. Heinrich, *Ships for the Seven Seas*, 68, 70–73, 75.
187. Farr and Bostick, *Shipbuilding at Cramp & Sons*, 21, 22.
188. Heinrich, *Ships for the Seven Seas*, 77, 80.
189. Fisher, "Maritime History of the Reading," 174, 179.
190. Rottenburg, *Man Who Made Wall Street*, 130, 163–65.
191. Fisher, "Maritime History of the Reading," 179–80; Heinrich, *Ships for the Seven Seas*, 81.
192. Jones, "Commodity Clause Legislation," 579, 588–89.

Chapter 16

193. Tute, *Atlantic Conquest*, 111–12.
194. Heinrich, *Ships for the Seven Seas*, 101–2, 104–7, 109.
195. Ibid., 38, 110–13, 115–21.
196. Potter and Nimitz, *Sea Power*, 366, 368, 374.
197. Heinrich, *Ships for the Seven Seas*, 122–23, 125–26, 152.
198. Daniel M. Dailey Collection, private collection.
199. Heinrich, *Ships for the Seven Seas*, 120, 139, 148–51, 154–55.
200. *Philadelphia Inquirer*, June 17, 1913; *New York Times*, June 17, 1913.
201. Heinrich, *Ships for the Seven Seas*, 170, 196–97; Farr and Bostick, *Shipbuilding at Cramp & Sons*, 13–14.

Epilogue

202. Heinrich, *Ships for the Seven Seas*, 49.
203. Maddocks, "Atlantic Crossing," 168.
204. Cope family papers, background note, 4.
205. Tute, *Atlantic Conquest*, 71–75.
206. Ibid., 87.

BIBLIOGRAPHY

AECOM. www.diggingi95.com.

Allen, David G. *James Rumsey, American Inventor*. West Virginia State Museum Education, 2008. wvstatemuseumed.wv.gov/assets/James_Rumsey_biography.pdf.

Bell, Daniel. *The End of Ideology: On the Exhaustion of Political Ideas in the Fifties*. Glencoe, IL: Free Press, 1960.

Bishop, J. Leander. *A History of American Manufactures, 1608–1860*. Philadelphia, PA: Edward Young & Company, 1868.

Bower, Samuel D.S. *Bower Family of Philadelphia, PA*. Philadelphia: Historical Society of Pennsylvania (HSP), 1858.

Brewington, Marion V. "Maritime Philadelphia 1609–1837." *Pennsylvania Magazine of History & Biography* 63, no. 2 (April 1939).

———. *Shipcarvers of North America*. New York: Dover Pub Inc., 1962.

Brewington, Marion V., comp. *Philadelphia Customs District: Vessel Data Taken from Surveyor's Certificates, Shipbuilder's & Master Carpenter's Certificates, 1793–1799*. Mystic Seaport, CT: G.W. Blunt White Library, circa 1940.

Bronner, Edwin B. "Indian Deed for Petty's Island." *Pennsylvania Magazine of History & Biography* 89 (January 1965).

Buell, Augustus C. *The Memoirs of Charles H. Cramp*. Philadelphia, PA: J.B. Lippincott Company, 1906.

Carousso, Dorothee Hughes. "Esther King of Philadelphia and Bucks Counties and Her Bowyer, Lynn and Elfreth Children." *Pennsylvania Genealogical Magazine* 24, no. 4 (1966).

Chandler, Charles Lyon. *Early Shipbuilding in Pennsylvania, 1683–1812*. Reprint. Philadelphia, PA: Guild of Brackett Lecturers, 1932.

Chapelle, Howard. *History of American Sailing Ships*. New York: W.W. Norton, 1935.

City Directories of Philadelphia, 1785–1870. Greater Philadelphia Geohistory Network. philageohistory.org.

Clark, Dennis. *The Irish in Philadelphia*. Philadelphia, PA: Temple University Press, 1973.

Colton, Tim. "Hillman Ship & Engine Building." U.S. Shipbuilding History/ Canadian Shipbuilding History. http://www.shipbuildinghistory.com/ shipyards/19thcentury/hillman.htm.

Cotter, John L., Daniel G. Roberts and Michael Parrington. *The Buried Past: An Archaeological History of Philadelphia*. Philadelphia: University of Pennsylvania Press, 1992.

Craig, Dr. Peter Stebbins. "Chronology." Colonial Swedes. colonialswedes.net/ chronology.

———. "Peter Gunnarsson Rambo." *Swedish Colonial Society Journal* (Fall 1990): 1–2.

Crowther, Simeon. "The Shipbuilding Output of the Delaware Valley, 1722– 1776." *Proceedings of American Philosophical Society* 117, no. 2 (April 10, 1973).

Daughan, George C. *If by Sea: The Forging of the American Navy—From the Revolution to the War of 1812*. New York: Basic Books, 2008.

The Dictionary of Ulster Biography. "John Grubb Richardson (1813–1890)." newulsterbiography.co.uk/index.php/home/viewPerson/1874/Richardson.

Digging 195. "Historical Context." diggingi95.com/project-information/historic-context.

Doerflinger, T.M. *A Vigorous Spirit of Enterprise*. Chapel Hill: University of North Carolina Press, 1986.

Dorwart, Jeffery M. *Invasion and Insurrection: Security, Defense, and War in the Delaware Valley, 1621–1815*. Newark: University of Delaware Press, 2008.

———. "Shipbuilding and Shipyards." Encyclopedia of Greater Philadelphia, 2013. Rutgers University. philadelphiaencyclopedia.org.

Duffield, Ulysses Grant. *The Neafie & Levy Ship and Engine Building Company (Penn Works)*. Philadelphia, PA: Franklin Printing Company, 1896.

Dunn, Mary Maples, and Richard Dunn. "The Founding, 1681–1701." In *Philadelphia: A 300 Year History*. Edited by Russell F. Weigley. New York: W.W. Norton, 1982.

Farley, James J. *To Commit Ourselves to Our Own Ingenuity: Joshua Humphreys—Early Philadelphia Shipbuilding*. E-book. http://earlyphiladelphiashipbuilding.wordpress. com

Farr, Gail E., and Brett F. Bostick. *Shipbuilding at Cramp & Sons: A History and Guide to Collections of the William Cramp & Sons Ship and Engine Building Company (1830– 1927) and the Cramp Shipbuilding Company (1941–46) of Philadelphia*. Philadelphia, PA: Philadelphia Maritime Museum, 1991.

Ferguson, Eugene S. *Oliver Evans: Inventive Genius of the American Industrial Revolution*. Greenville, DE: Hagley Museum and Library, 1980.

Fisher, Barbara. "Maritime History of the Reading, 1833–1905." *Pennsylvania Magazine of History & Biography* 86 (April 1962).

Gauer, David W. *Vaughan Shipwrights of Kensington, Philadelphia, Their Van Hook & Norris Lineages and Combined Progeny*. Decorah, IA: Anundsen Pub. Company, 1982.

Geffen, Elizabeth M. "Industrial Development and Social Crisis, 1841–1854." In *Philadelphia: A 300 Year History*. Edited by Russell F. Weigley. New York: W.W. Norton, 1982.

Gelber, Harry G. *The Dragon and the Foreign Devils: China and the World, 1100 B.C. to the Present*. London: Bloomsbury Publishing, 2007.

Gillingham, Harold E. "Some Colonial Ships Built in Philadelphia." *Pennsylvania Magazine of History & Biography* 56 (April 1932).

Goldenburg, Joseph A. *Shipbuilding in Colonial America*. Charlottesville: University Press of Virginia, 1976.

Goldstein, Jonathan. *Philadelphia and the China Trade, 1682–1846: Commercial, Cultural, and Attitudinal Effects*. University Park: Pennsylvania State University Press, 1978.

Hardy, Charles, III. "Fish or Foul: A History of the Delaware River Basin through the Perspective of the American Shad, 1682 to the Present." *Pennsylvania History* 66, no. 4 (1999): 511–12.

Harrison, Eliza Cope. *Philadelphia Merchant: The Diary of Thomas P. Cope, 1800–1851*. South Bend, IN: Gateway Editions, 1978.

Heinrich, Thomas R. *Ships for the Seven Seas: Philadelphia Shipbuilding in the Age of Industrial Capitalism*. Baltimore, MD: Johns Hopkins University Press, 1997.

Helffenstein, Abraham Ernest. *Pierre Fauconnier and His Descendants: With Some Account of the Allied Valleaux*. Philadelphia, PA: S.H. Burbank, 1911.

Henry, William Wirt. *Eminent and Representative Men of Virginia and the District of Columbia in the Nineteenth Century: With a Concise Historical Sketch of Virginia*. Madison, WI: Brant & Fuller, 1893.

Hopkinson, Francis. *The Miscellaneous Essays and Occasional Writings of Francis Hopkinson Esq.* Vol. 2. Philadelphia, PA: T. Dobson, 1792.

Hoyt, Helen P. "The Wreck of the 'Philosopher' Helvetius." *Hawaiian Journal of History* 2, no. 4 (1968).

Hurd, D. Hamilton. *History of New London County, Connecticut, with Biographical Sketches of Many of Its Pioneers and Prominent Men*. Philadelphia, PA: J.W. Lewis & Company, 1882.

Iles, George. *Leading American Inventors*. New York: Henry Holt and Company, 1912.

Illick, Joseph E. *Colonial Pennsylvania—A History*. New York: Charles Scribner's Sons, 1976.

In Search of Nothing. "History 101." https://section106.wordpress.com/history-101.

Jackson, Claude. *A Maritime History and Survey of the Cape Fear and Northeast Cape Fear Rivers, Wilmington Harbor, North Carolina*. Wilmington, NC: U.S. Army Corps of Engineers, Wilmington District, 1996.

Jackson, John W. *The Pennsylvania Navy, 1775–1781: The Defense of the Delaware*. New Brunswick, NJ: Rutgers University Press, 1974.

Jones, Eliot. "The Commodity Clause Legislation and the Anthracite Railroads." *Quarterly Journal of Economics* 27, no. 4 (August 1913): 579, 588–89.

Jordan, John W. *Colonial and Revolutionary Families of Pennsylvania*. New York: Lewis Publishing Company, 1911.

Jordan, John W., Thomas Lynch Montgomery, Ernest Spofford and Frederic Antes Godcharles. *Encyclopedia of Pennsylvania Biography*. Vol. 15. New York: Lewis Historical Pub. Company, 1924.

Keyser, Peter D. "Colonel Jehu Eyre," *Pennsylvania Magazine of History & Biography* 3 (1879): 418.

Klein, Phillip S., and Ari Hoogenboom. *A History of Pennsylvania*. University Park: Pennsylvania State University Press, 1973.

Kyriakodis, Harry. *Philadelphia's Lost Waterfront*. Charleston, SC: The History Press, 2011.

Laing, Alexander. *Seafaring America*. New York: American Heritage Publishing Company, 1974.

Leach, Frank Willing. Genealogical data and correspondence relating to old Philadelphia families printed in the *North American*, June 9, 1912, and "The Old Eyre House" in the *Evening Bulletin*, July 1, 1911. Historical Society of Pennsylvania Collections, Gen Le 17.

Maddocks, Melvin. "The Atlantic Crossing." In *The Seafarers*. Alexandria, VA: Time-Life Books, 1980.

The Maritime Heritage Project. "Steamships, Ship Passengers and Sea Captains: San Francisco, 1846–1900." https://www.maritimeheritage.org/ships/steamships.html.

McCarthy, Jack. *In the Cradle of Industry and Liberty: A History of Manufacturing in Philadelphia*. San Antonio, TX: HPNbooks, 2016.

Milano, Kenneth. *History of Penn Treaty Park*. Charleston, SC: The History Press, 2009.

———. *Palmer Cemetery and the Historic Burial Grounds of Kensington & Fishtown*. Charleston, SC: The History Press, 2011.

———. "Samuel Bower's Shipyards at Point Pleasant, Kensington, 1789–1830." Blog post. The Mariners' Museum Online Catalog, March 28, 2008. catalogs.marinersmuseum.org/object/CL7002.

———. *Supplement to the History of the Kensington Soup Society: Comprising Biographies of the Founders*. Lancaster, PA: Brenneman Printing Inc., 2009.

Miller, Donald L., and Richard E. Sharpless. *The Kingdom of Coal: Work, Enterprise, and Ethnic Communities in the Mine Fields*. Philadelphia: University of Pennsylvania Press, 1985.

Miller, Randall M., and William A. Pencak, eds. *Pennsylvania: A History of the Commonwealth*. University Park: Pennsylvania State University Press, 2002.

Miller, Richard G. "The Federal City, 1783–1800." In *Philadelphia: A 300 Year History*. Edited by Russell F. Weigley. New York: W.W. Norton, 1982.

Nash, Gary B. *First City: Philadelphia and the Forging of Historical Memory*. Philadelphia: University of Pennsylvania Press, 2001.

Online Archive of California. "A Guide to the Union Cargo Manifests." 1831, 1851. oac.cdlib.org.

Potter, E.B., and Chester W. Nimitz. *Sea Power—A Naval History*. Englewood Cliffs, NJ: Prentice-Hall Inc., 1960.

Remer, Rich. "Fishtown and the Shad Fisheries." *Pennsylvania Legacies* 2, no. 2 (November 2002): 20.

———. "Old Kensington." *PA Legacies* 2, no. 2 (November 2002): 8–9.

Remer, Rich, and Ken Milano. "Kensington and the Founding of Philadelphia (1681–1800)." In *Kensington History: Stories and Memories*. Edited by Jamie Catrambone and Harry C. Silcox. Philadelphia, PA: Brighton Press, 1996.

Richardson, Edgar P. "The Athens of America, 1800–1825." In *Philadelphia: A 300 Year History*. Edited by Russell F. Weigley. New York: W.W. Norton, 1982.

Ridgely-Nevitt, Cedric. *American Steamships on the Atlantic*. Newark: University of Delaware Press, 1981.

Robson, Charles, ed. *Biographical Encyclopaedia of Pennsylvania of the Nineteenth Century*. Philadelphia, PA: Galaxy Publishing, 1874.

Rosen, William. *The Most Powerful Idea in the World: A Story of Steam, Industry and Invention*. Chicago: University of Chicago Press, 2010.

Rottenburg, Dan. *The Man Who Made Wall Street: Anthony Drexel and the Rise of Modern Finance*. Philadelphia: University of Pennsylvania Press, 2001.

Scharf, J. Thomas, and Thompson Westcott. *History of Philadelphia, 1609–1884*. Philadelphia, PA: L.H. Everts, 1884.

Silverman, Sharon Hernes. "History Lessons from the Morton Homestead." *Pennsylvania Heritage Magazine* 25, no. 1 (Winter 1999).

Soderlund, Jean. *Lenape Country: Delaware Valley Society Before William Penn*. Philadelphia: University of Pennsylvania Press, 2014.

Steiner, Linda. "Pennsylvania Fishes." Pennsylvania Fish and Boat Commission. fishandboat.com/Fish/PennsylvaniaFishes/GalleryPennsylvaniaFishes/Pages/Herrings.aspx.

Sutcliffe, Andrea. *Steam: The Untold Story of America's First Great Invention*. New York: Palgrave Macmillan, 2004.

Tanner, Henry. *Stranger's Guide*. Philadelphia, PA: H.S. Tanner, 1830. loc.gov/item/78694442.

Thompson, Peter. "The Iron & Steel Shipbuilding Data Set, 1825–1914: Sources, Coverage, & Coding Decisions." FIO Digital Commons, Florida International University Research, 2008. digitalcommons.fiu.edu.

Tute, Warren. *Atlantic Conquest: The Men and Ships of the Glorious Age of Steam*. Boston: Little, Brown & Company, 1962.

U.S. Department of the Treasury. "Steam-Engines: Letter from the Secretary of Treasury, Transmitting, in Obedience to a Resolution of the House, of the 29th of June Last, Information in Relation to Steam Engines, etc." N.p.: Thomas Allen, printer, 1838.

Van Deusen, Captain Albert Harrison. *Van Deursen Family*. Vols. 1 and 2. New York: Frank Allaben Genealogical Company, 1912.

Wainwright, Nicholas. "The Age of Nicholas Biddle, 1825–1841." In *Philadelphia: A 300 Year History*. Edited by Russell F. Weigley. New York: W.W. Norton, 1982.

Walther, Rudolph J. *Happenings in Ye Olde Philadelphia, 1680–1900*. Philadelphia, PA: Walther Printing House, 1925.

Warner, Sam Bass. *The Private City: Philadelphia in Three Periods of Its Growth.* Philadelphia: University of Pennsylvania Press, 1987.

Watson, John F. *Annals of Philadelphia and Pennsylvania, in the Olden Time; Being a Collection of Memoirs, Anecdotes, and Incidents.* Vol. 2. New York: John Pennington and Uriah Hunt, 1857.

Weightman, Gavin. *The Industrial Revolutionaries: The Making of the Modern World, 1776–1914.* New York: Grove Press, 2007.

Weslager, C.A. *New Sweden on the Delaware.* Wilmington, DE: Middle Atlantic Press, 1988.

Whipple, A.B.C. "The Clipper Ships." In *The Seafarers.* Alexandria, VA: Time-Life Books, 1980.

Wokeck, Marianne S. *Trade in Strangers: The Beginnings of Mass Migration to North America.* University Park: Pennsylvania State University Press, 1999.

Yamin, Rebecca. *Digging in the City of Brotherly Love: Stories from Philadelphia Archaeology.* New Haven, CT: Yale University Press, 2008.

INDEX

A

Allaire, Alexander 31, 33
American Steamship Company 98, 99,
    107, 110

B

Baker, John 28, 29
Baldwin Locomotive Works 118
Baldwin, Matthias 69
Ball, Joseph 53, 60, 69
Ball, William 26
Beideman, Jacob 50, 68
Benjamin Fairman 33
Birely
    Birely, Hillman & Streaker 93, 101
    Birely, Jacob 75, 88, 93, 110, 113
    Birely, John 7, 50, 59, 67, 68, 72, 74,
        84, 93
    Birely & Lynn 88
    Birely & Son 78, 79
    Birely & Tees 75
    Birely, Theodore 69, 78, 79, 80, 93
Black Ball Line 56
Boulton & Watt 39

Bower
    Bower, Joseph 38, 41, 43, 52, 65
    Bower, Joshua 58
    Bower, Samuel 45, 46, 52, 65
    Bower & Van Dusen 58
    Bower & Vaughan 52, 57, 67
    Bower, William 37, 43
Bowyer, John 25
Brown, Peter 41
Brusstar, Samuel 38, 46

C

Cassel, Nicholas 29, 31
City Ice Boat 69, 81
Clyde Line 97, 98, 101, 107, 114
Clyde, William 97, 101, 109
Cock, Lasse 20, 21
Cock, Peter 20
Consolidation of Philadelphia 84, 87
Cope
    Cope Line 58, 68, 81, 119
    Henry and Alfred (H&A) 81, 119
    Thomas P 56, 68, 119
Corsair II 109
cotton 51, 56, 101

Cramp
  Cramp, Charles 68, 72, 74, 81, 89, 97, 98, 99, 101, 106, 110, 113, 114, 115, 122
  Cramp, Martin 50
  Cramp, Peter 71
  Cramp & Sons 98, 99
  Cramp, William 7, 59, 67, 68, 71, 72, 74, 82, 88, 92, 99, 110, 116, 118, 119

D

Dennis, Henry 30
Dennis, Richard 38
Drexel, Anthony 104
Drexel, Morgan & Company 104, 105
Dutch West India Company 18

E

Elfreth, Jeremiah 30, 32
Elfreth, Josiah 25
Empress of China 43
Ericsson, John 67
Evans, Oliver 39, 40, 47, 48, 49, 57
Eyre
  Eyre, Benjamin 36, 38
  Eyre, Franklin 56, 67
  Eyre, George, Jr. 43, 52
  Eyre, George, Sr. 33, 56
  Eyre, Jehu, Sr. 34, 35
  Eyre, Jehu W. 67
  Eyre, Manuel 34, 35, 42, 44

F

Fairman, Benjamin 30
Fairman Mansion 26, 69
Fairman, Thomas 21, 22, 25, 26, 28
Fitch, John 39, 40, 47
Franklin Iron Works 84

G

General Greene 36, 38
Girard, Stephen 43, 52
Goff, Morris 38, 43
Gowen, Franklin 96
Grice
  Grice, Francis, Jr. 84
  Grice, Francis (machinist) 83
  Grice, Francis, Sr. 12, 38, 42, 55, 57, 82
  Grice, Joseph, Jr. 57
  Grice, Joseph, Sr. 41, 43, 52, 57
  Grice, Samuel 59, 69, 70, 71, 83
  Grice, Samuel B. 46, 83, 84, 88, 93
Griscom, Clement 107, 110
Guerriere 55
Gunners Run 25

H

Hamburg-America Line 121
Hammitt, John H. 107
Hammitt, John K. 7, 67, 75, 76, 86, 87
Hastings, Samuel 30
Hayes, William 30
Helvetius 43
Hillman, Charles 88, 110
Hillman & Sons 110, 113
Holloway, Thomas 61, 70
Holme, Thomas 21
Humphreys, Joshua 24, 45, 99

I

iceboats 69
Imperial Russian Navy 101, 114
Industrial Revolution 39, 59, 69, 121
Inman Line 98, 107
Inman, William 97, 98
International Navigation Company 98, 107, 110, 114
I.P. Morris & Company 72, 118
Ironsides 89, 113

J

James T. Sutton & Company. *See* Sutton, James T.
Jupiter 116

K

Kalmar Nyckel 18, 19
Kensington Screw Dock 65, 87
Kinsey, Elizabeth 21
Kinsey, John 20

L

Landell, George 52, 81
Large, Daniel 57
Lehigh Coal & Navigation Company 60, 69
Lenni-Lenape 15, 16
Levy, Edmund 93, 110
Levy, John 61, 72, 86, 93
Loper, Captain Richard F. 61, 72, 74, 78, 79, 80, 84
Luckenbach, Lewis 105
Lynn
  Lynn, John W. 88, 89, 95
  Lynn, Joseph (first gen) 25, 27
  Lynn, Joseph (second gen) 25, 27, 30, 32
  Lynn, Joseph (third gen) 33, 41, 46, 53
  Lynn, Matthew 75
  Lynn, Michael 58

M

Markham, William 21
Mars Works 49, 57
Masters, Thomas 28
McLeod, Archibald 104
Merrick, Samuel 7
  Merrick & Sons Southwark 89
Merrick & Towne 61, 67, 69, 88

Miller, Henry 68
Montesquieu 43
Morgan, J. Pierpont 104, 105, 109
Morris, I.P. 61, 81, 89, 106
  Port Richmond Iron Foundry 110

N

Neafie
  Neafie, Jacob 61, 72, 86, 93, 97, 110, 116
  Reaney, Neafie & Levy 72
Norris
  Norris, Isaac 26, 27, 28
  Norris, John, Jr. 42, 44, 46
  Norris, John, Sr. 28, 29, 32
  Norris, Joseph 46
  Norris, Thomas 29, 46

O

Ogborn, John 30, 31, 34
Oldman, Joseph 30

P

Palmer, Anthony 7, 15, 26, 28, 29, 60
Parrock, James 27, 29, 30
Passyunk 16, 20
Penn Steam Engine & Boiler Works 72. *See* Reaney, Neafie & Levy
Pennsylvania Railroad 65, 96, 98, 99, 107, 110, 121
Penrose, Bartholomew 24
Penrose, Thomas 27
Philadelphia Navy Yard 55, 67, 89
Philadelphia & Reading Railroad 60, 72, 89, 95, 101, 102. *See* Richmond branch
Point Pleasant 28, 38, 52, 57, 69, 75, 81
Port Richmond Iron Foundry 110. *See also* Morris, I.P.
Port Richmond Terminal 72, 96, 99, 106

R

Rambo, Gunnar 21, 25
Rambo, Peter 19
Reaney, Neafie & Levy 72, 80, 86
Reaney, Thomas 72, 96
Red "D" Line 76, 107
Red Star Line 107
Reiss, Johan Georg 28, 29, 50
Retvizan 115
Rice, Johan Georg 29. *See also* Reiss,
    Johan Georg
Rice, William 29, 32
Richmond branch 60
Robinson, Moncure 60
Rousseau 43

S

Samuel S. Lewis 78, 79, 84
shad 7, 16, 28, 29, 50, 59
Shreeve family 31, 33
Spencer, John 29
Stanton, Thomas P. and J.W. 80
Star of the South 78, 80, 84
Streaker, David 88, 110
Sutton
    Sutton, James T. 70, 84
    Sutton, William 7, 67, 71, 84, 93

T

Tees
    Tees, Jacob 58, 68, 69, 70, 88
    Tees, Samuel 58
    Tees Van Hook, Bower & Van Dusen
    58
Towne, John 61, 89

U

USS *New Ironsides* 89
USS *New York* 110, 113, 114

V

Van Dusen
    Van Dusen & Birely 69, 70
    Van Dusen, Joseph Ball 69
    Van Dusen, Matthew, Jr. 58, 88
    Van Dusen, Matthew, Sr. 52, 53
    Van Dusen, Nicholas 53, 69
    Van Dusen, Washington 69
Van Hook
    Van Hook, Henry 45, 53
    Van Hook, William 54, 58
Vaughan
    John Vaughan & Bower 57, 67
    John Vaughan & Son 69, 70, 75
    Vaughan, Griffith 44
    Vaughan, Harmon Stout 86
    Vaughan, Jacob Keen 75, 88
    Vaughan, John 7, 54, 56, 58, 68, 69,
      70, 75
    Vaughan & Lynn 80, 81, 86
    Vaughan & Son 68
    Vaughan, Thomas, Jr. 45, 46, 52, 53,
      58
    Vaughan, Thomas, Sr. 44, 45
    Vaughan, William 45
    Vaughan, William B. 54
Voigt, Henry 40
Voltaire 43

W

Watt, James 39
West, Charles 27, 28
West, James 23, 24, 33
White, Isaac 43, 52
Wilmington, Delaware 18, 98, 122
Wilson, John 41
Wright, Richard 31, 33

Z

Zabiaca 101

ABOUT THE AUTHOR

Gretchen M. Bell is a writer and researcher in Philadelphia, Pennsylvania. Gretchen is an active member of the Philadelphia Ship Preservation Guild and the Society for Industrial Archeology's local Oliver Evans Chapter. Gretchen has worked with maritime organizations as a research assistant and continues to collaborate with local organizations and individuals to preserve the maritime history of Philadelphia.

Visit us at
www.historypress.com